Anonymous

Glimpses in America

The New World as We Saw It

Anonymous

Glimpses in America
The New World as We Saw It

ISBN/EAN: 9783744693745

Printed in Europe, USA, Canada, Australia, Japan

Cover: Foto ©Thomas Meinert / pixelio.de

More available books at **www.hansebooks.com**

GLIMPSES IN AMERICA;

OR,

THE NEW WORLD AS WE SAW IT.

WITH

NOTICES OF THE EVANGELICAL ALLIANCE, THE
PACIFIC RAILWAY, AND CALIFORNIA.

BY THE

AUTHOR OF "LIFE'S TRUE BEATITUDE."

LONDON:
PUBLISHED FOR THE AUTHOR AT THE
WESLEYAN CONFERENCE OFFICE,
2, CASTLE STREET, CITY ROAD;
SOLD AT 66, PATERNOSTER ROW.
1875.

PREFACE.

THIS volume is not a diary, nor is it a book of travel. It is certainly very much of the nature of both. Yet it is not exactly either; for it eschews the inevitable egotism of the one, and the inherent, and often dry and enfeebling, details of the other.

Indeed, the work is just what it says it is,—a series of glimpses,—of glimpses caught, not with the eyes of others, nor through the too often obfuscating *media* of other people's lucubrations, but caught with our own eyes, and reproduced with as much exactness as scenes and events transferred with fidelity to writing usually have.

Should any one ask why the book has been written, our answer is ready. Some books have been written to inform, some to amuse, and some to edify; but this has been written to accomplish all three. With what success, our readers will judge.

DUNDALK, 1875.

CONTENTS.

CHAPTER I.

TO THE OTHER SIDE OF THE ATLANTIC.

WHAT a beautiful morning!—so still, so genial, and withal so cheerful with the song of birds, and with the clear yet mellow radiance of an early autumn sun. Yet we confess to a feeling of sadness; for, with a thoughtful sense of the changeful and uncertain nature of all things mortal, we are leaving friends, and home, and native land.

The morning meal, quickly despatched, is followed by a hasty adieu to those we love, and soon after six o'clock we are sitting in a train that steams swiftly and smoothly 'twixt green and yellow fields, and by quiet farmsteads, whose drowsy inmates are scarcely yet astir. But as we proceed, the day changes, giving us clouds and murky mists, and pattering rain instead of sunshine; and at 10 a.m., amid falling showers, and streaming and muddy streets, we find ourselves in the old and far-famed city of Cork.

A few hours after we are on our way to Queenstown, where we arrive at 5 p.m. Soon our luggage is safely stowed away in the office of the steamship company, and ourselves in the Queen's Hotel; and, having supped with an old acquaintance, who, in glowing words, has told us much of America, its cities, its people, and its social customs, we retire

early, with the desire to get a good night's rest ere
we are, on the morrow, tossed and sick amid the
rocking of the waves.

Next morning we are gladdened by the intelligence
that our keys—which we had forgotten, and the want
of which made us feel awkward and uncomfortable—
had arrived by the post, and, breakfast being over,
we get off to the steam-packet office, there to await
the arrival of our ship, which had left Liverpool on
the previous day. At 1 p.m. she is sighted from the
office ; which fact being announced to us, we, with a
good many other passengers, chiefly steerage, get
aboard the tender, which quickly steams for the big
ship that awaits our arrival in the offing beyond
the bay. ·

And what an unpleasant little trip,—rain falling,
wind squally, sea cranky, and ever and anon covering
us with showers of briny and chilling spray, while our
little craft is rocking, and rolling, and dipping, as if
anxious to give us an admonitory foretaste of what
awaits us on the deep.

But we are soon on board the smoking leviathan,
where we find agreeable officers, about 100 saloon
passengers, and comfortable quarters in the captain's
state room, which has been kindly allotted to us for
the voyage.

And this voyage, now that it is past, why need we
use many words in describing it ? It was like what
such voyages usually are, and which have been
described a thousand and one times over ; without
any specially unfavourable weather, though gales were

sometimes stiff, and waves high; without any unusual quantity of sea-sickness ; and without any casualties, save that one poor woman in the steerage, a Swede, going to join her husband in America, died, and was buried in the deep, and a gentleman had his leg broken by a fall caused by the unexpected and heavy rolling of the ship. As for ourselves, we were generally well, though sometimes troubled with a most disagreeable nausea, and, on one or two occasions, were fairly sick.

The fare was abundant, but not of the first quality. Many of our fellow-voyagers were Americans of the Yankee type, who had been at the Vienna Exhibition, and who, having "done Europe," had much to say of the superiority of Americans to all other mortals else. Perhaps they were right; but we should have thought much more of them but for their smoking, chewing, spitting, and scarcely intermittent card-playing, all of which they seemed to regard as essential accomplishments of highly civilised life. Yet they were, on the whole, very agreeable people ; and, though less taciturn, I doubt if they were at all more egotistic than were some English gentlemen that were on board, whose national vanity they sometimes peppered by playfully bantering the characteristic failings which Americans in general ascribe to "Johnny Bull."

During the voyage two Sundays intervened, upon which we had Divine Service, the captain assisting by reading prayers. We often, when at meals especially, had some conversation on matters of theological controversy, that sometimes excited anger and sometimes mirth ; but few were disposed to enter seriously on the subject of personal religion, or to speak about religion as a *power* to renovate the heart and to rectify and elevate the life. Many were more or less poisoned with infidel notions ; and one American, returning in broken health from Paris, and who sat near us at meals, was, so far as one could judge from his talk and temper, a bitter Atheist. By the way, this sour unbeliever had a little cylinder-shaped wife, whose temper and appetite seemed never to fail. "What a bundle of sunshine is that little woman," observed an American lady, who, no doubt, thought the description strikingly poetic. But, as we had never seen sunshine in bundles, we failed to see the aptness of the metaphor ; and, though we could heartily appreciate the good temper and patience of this amiable woman, we found it impossible to abstain from contrasting in our thoughts the ethereal nature of light with the stout little body who could despatch with indescribable ease, gusto, and speed, a beef-steak, ham, chicken, and eggs at breakfast, and a quantity of sundries at dinner that might perceptibly add to the rotund protuberance of a London alderman.

But, to us, the most interesting person in the company was a venerable American D.D. He was a genuine gentleman, and a man of rich and extensive theological and literary knowledge ; and, moreover, he knew from personal observation almost every rare and curious thing, and every place ; for he had travelled the world all over, and was now returning with the purpose of ending his earthly pilgrimage in the land of his birth. He was conversant, too, with " the deep things of God," for he had been a Christian from his youth, and a Christian minister during the best years of his life. How delightful it was to hear this patriarchal man talk either of persons and places in America, or of his visits to France, Switzerland, and Italy, or of his travels in Egypt, Arabia, and the Holy Land ; or to hear him expound some theological controversy, or converse on experimental religion ; or to hear him cut and chop with his keen logic, or wither with his quiet and half-playful sarcasm the absurd nostrums of Rationalistic, Socinian, or Pantheistic unbelievers. Some of his anecdotes were exceedingly racy, of which the following may be suggestive to some pious people, who, with prudent regard for their own purses, very honestly imagine that Christian ministers should labour hard, and yet subsist on such essences as sustain the inhabitants of heaven. "A church," said this old man, "in need of a pastor, waited by deputation on a venerable minister, for the purpose of asking his advice as to whom they should choose. They dwelt long and eloquently on the many and estimable qualities of the person who would suit them : saying he must be a good scholar, an eloquent preacher, a self-denying and indefatigable pastor, with many other admirable et ceteras ; but they added, ' You know, Mr. A——, we are a very poor people, and the utmost we can afford to pay our minister is four hundred dollars a year.' ' Hem ! ' said the old gentleman, looking at

them wisely, 'I know of only one man who would
suit you.' This announcement delighted them, and
they waited in eager expectation of hearing his name.
'That man,' added he, 'is Doctor Dwight. You
know he is a long while dead; but he has now been
so many years in heaven that, *perhaps*, if you can
get him, he may be able to live on four hundred
dollars a year.' It is needless to add with what feelings of pious disgust these large-hearted representatives of the church withdrew."

Sunday, the 7th September, Divine Service in the
saloon being ended, and luncheon over, our attention
is attracted by the excitement of several persons on
deck. They have caught sight of the pilot-boat, and,
peering through their glasses, are eagerly watching
her approach. A few hours, and the pilot is in
charge of our steamer, and all are joyfully anti-
cipating a safe landing in New York on the following
day. And so it turns out.

In the morning the low shores of Long Island are
in view, and by 2 p.m., amid placid waters, bright
sunshine, and many mutual congratulations, we steam
into the spacious and beautiful bay upon whose verge
is seated the empire city of the West. Beautiful
indeed this bay is; shut in by winding shores and
gently sloping hills, that are everywhere dotted with
stately mansions and villas nestling in foliage that
seems as yet untouched by the yellow finger of
declining autumn, and surrounded by gardens whose
terraced slopes are gay with variegated floral bloom.
Just in front are jutting piers, bristling with a dense

array of masts that are adorned with the colours of many nations; and beyond lies the great city itself, with its deep, massive, and huge piles. of building, and surmounted by many shooting spires and broad-expanding domes that stand out in conspicuous relief upon the exquisitely clear and azure sky. Around us the waters seem in every direction instinct with life ;—white-sailed yachts, hissing tugs, ponderous, palace-looking ferry-boats, propelled by steam ; outward bound ships, homeward bound ships, ships of all imaginable shapes and sizes, and on all imaginable errands, are flitting hither and thither, like flies that shoot, and sail, and sport upon our pools in summer.

But what a shame it is to deface and mar the beauty of such a picture by sticking in conspicuous places on the sloping hills huge advertisements,—in great, staring, painted or whitewashed letters,—of newspapers, "Rising Sun Stove Polish," "Vinegar Bitters," and such like ! Indeed, this often offends the eye in the American landscape ; indicating the utilitarian nature of our cousins, and their never-failing appreciation of the all-important dollar.

After some delay we are conveyed from our ship by steam-tug to one of the multitudinous wooden piers of which we have already spoken. Here polite Custom-house officials overhaul and pass our baggage; after which we rumble in a ponderous four-wheeled machine, called a carriage, to our hotel in Broadway, where we are well provided for at a most respectable charge.

But, oh! what quantities of Virginian weed must

be consumed in this place! Clouds of tobacco smoke, exsquirted saliva, and quantities of soiled spittoons crammed with bits of cigars and used-up quids, and variegated with defunct bottle-corks and discoloured apple rind, produce such an effect upon nose, eyes, and stomach as we need not stay to explain.

The beds, however, are comfortable, the food is ample and palatable, and everything is served up in a style most grateful to one who has been long inwardly disquieted by steamboat smells, and by uneasy tossings on old Neptune's wave.

CHAPTER II.

NEW YORK CITY.

FATIGUE slept off, and feeling tolerably well after our American breakfast of ice-water, tea, hot rolls, butter, chop—with surroundings of hominy, buckwheat cake, potatoes, pickles, golden syrup, &c., which we failed to appreciate—we stroll from our hotel along the side-walk in Broadway. The blue sky is clear, lofty, and cloudless, and the bright sun is much hotter than it usually is during the midsummer of our Emerald Isle. Great numbers of people hurry by us, all of whom are well dressed, and in garments not unlike our own, save that wherever the eye turns it meets the neat, turned-down shirt collar, well-adjusted neck-tie, and broad, white, staring shirt front, with, albeit the weather is so hot, an occasional light overcoat hanging loosely on shoulders that have been amply supplemented by the crafty padding of the tailor's art. Goatees and moustaches are not so numerous as we had anticipated, for many male faces are effeminately shaven ; but a dandy cane, a showy ring, a sparkling gold watch-guard, and a cigar seem to be the inalienable birthright of almost the humblest American-born citizen.

The ladies we meet are smart, neat, and fashionable, and evidently given to jewelry, silks, and laces ;

which, considering the high price of these articles in America, are worn in wondrous profusion. It strikes us, too, that our fair cousins have a tinge of haughtiness in their expression and bearing of which they might with advantage be rid, and that, in general, they are smaller, paler, and better figures than women in the old country usually are. And here let me say that my subsequent observation led me to conclude that the American women, notwithstanding their love of display, which, indeed, seems a national weakness, are such admirable housekeepers as can scarcely be equalled elsewhere ; while many of them in good social positions work hard with their own hands, and make everything in and about their homes clean, comfortable, and attractively bright.

Of the streets and buildings it is needless to give any description here, as information on these matters is sufficiently widely diffused. Let it suffice to say that we found, as indeed we expected to find, the city built on Manhattan Island, and consisting almost wholly of avenues and streets—the avenues running parallel with the length of the island, and lined with lofty and well-built houses, many of which are faced with brown stone or ornamental iron painted white, while the streets, in many cases equally handsome, form what the New Yorkers call blocks by, at brief and regular intervals, cutting the avenues at right angles. This arrangement of thoroughfares, which, by the way, characterises all American cities, is common-sense and convenient, enabling a stranger to find his way anywhere with little or no trouble, and contrasting very favourably with the irregular and, in many instances, narrow and dirty windings and twistings and oblique divergences of many of our cities at home. The shade-trees too, everywhere seen along the side-walks, strike one as being picturesque and refreshing, though the number of funereal-looking willows seem sadly suggestive of the mortality that is ever present even amid the busiest and gayest scenes of human life.

The finest buildings in New York are its insurance offices and its churches, though it has also some splendid monster hotels, public markets, and railway depots. As fires, like almost everything else in America, are on a large scale, the insurance companies do a thriving business, the profits of which exhibit themselves in the many lofty, spacious, and expensively-decorated offices that present their bold and elaborately-ornamented fronts in Broadway.

In praise of the New York Fire Brigade, which passes us in the street, it is impossible to say too much. It is beautiful to look upon, reminding us of a well-appointed train of British artillery; while engines, hose, escapes, horses, and men seem equal to any emergency that the Promethean element may possibly create.

But here, in a cross street, betwixt Broadway and Fourth Avenue, a regiment of the City Militia, or National Guard, is assembled for a "march out." They are Germans; for in this country each nationality, whether French, German, Italian, or Irish, is represented by its own volunteer or militia corps.

Now this German corps is somewhat curious and amusing to look at. What quantities of officers compared with the number of rank and file ! and what a display of plumes, gold lace, and middling-looking but richly-caparisoned chargers ! What gay talking in the ranks, what inattentive attention, and what hesitating and clumsy attempts at manual exercise ! But here are good face and figure, intelligence and manliness—just the sort of stuff out of which to manufacture an army, if need be. And now that they file off into Fourth Avenue, the music is really fine and soul-stirring, and the marching is good.

From what we have observed upon this and similar occasions, and from what we have seen of the systematic drilling of youth in the public schools, we have not been able to resist the conviction that the Americans, notwithstanding their love of commercial and similar industrial pursuits, are destined to become a military people ; but whether, in a country so vast, and with sometimes strongly-conflicting parties and interests, they shall turn their arms against each other or against foreigners, who can tell ? May our inference be wrong ! For who that loves liberty, truth, and progressive civilisation would wish to see great Columbia imitating, in their military ambition, their armaments, and their bloody and devastating wars, the nations of Continental Europe ? Or who with a spark of humanity in his soul would like again to see America involved in such a fratricidal struggle as lately brought convulsive agony to almost every part of her land, and anguish and desolation to multitudes of her once happy homes ?

A walk through Union Square, Madison Square, Washington Square, and others is an agreeable treat. All are in the heart of the city, and are at all times open to the people, having neither gates, railings, nor an obstructive police. Comfortable and ornamental seats are everywhere to be had, upon which the loiterer, however poor, may rest. Here he may regale himself with the sight of shrub and flower and artificial fount, that shoots its crystal jet towards the calm, clear dome above ; or with the chirping and chattering and flitting of sparrows, whose rights are jealously guarded against the rude assaults of truant boys, and for whom the civic authorities have provided little ornamental houses in the branching forks of shady trees ; or with the smart equipages that roll and clatter to and fro upon the distant pavement ; or with the still more distant stream of busy people that crowd the footways, like a picturesque and animated fringe upon the edges of the square.

But we must not linger, but hurry on to Central Park. Our way is through Fifth Avenue. And what a picture this long-drawn thoroughfare presents as we glance forward between its stately rows of luxurious-looking buildings ! What costly and extravagant grandeur everywhere meets the eye ! One could almost wish for an American Horace, who, like the Venusian bard, might compose an ode *in sui sœculi luxuriam*, that our transatlantic cousins might, perchance, halt in their career of wasteful and sinful expenditure, and ask themselves the question, In what is all this to end ? Palace-like houses line the way on either hand, with ever and anon churches, whose massive towers and tapering spires break and rise above the lofty outlines of the stately housetops. And what carriages !—an unbroken stream on either side, some speeding to the Park and others returning from it—of various shape and size, but all lightly and beautifully built, and drawn by handsomely-harnessed horses of sprightly gait and mien and noble form—and filled, too, with gay and fashionably-attired citizens. Nor does the extravagant display on the side-walks escape our notice ; for here there is such a show of dress as makes brocaded silks, costly laces, velvets, feathers, flowers, and sparkling jewelry seem almost as commonplace as foliage in a vernal wood.

The Park itself is really magnificent, covering an area of nearly 1,000 acres. Its undulating and, terraced slopes, winding avenues, broad and beautifully smooth carriage-drives ; its majestic trees, varied and extensive shrubberies, and ornamental flower-grounds ; its clear lake, fringed with tender green, upon whose bosom sail snowy swans, and whose waters are skimmed by sportive bird or swiftly-paddled skiff ; its curiously-designed and elaborately-embossed fountains and sky-besprinkling jets ; its noble statues and busts of gifted men ; its sweet and dreamy music, discoursed by minstrels for whom has been erected a costly and handsome stand : all combine to produce such effects upon the senses, the imagination, and the emotions, as make one almost suppose himself the dreaming and yet delighted victim of some sweet illusion, some soul-enthralling spell.

But the pleasure of the scene—mortal as we are— gives way to the pangs of hunger which now begin to importune us with imperative appeal; and, hurry- ing from the witching place of our rapt emotions, we are soon settled quietly down in a rather imposing restaurant. Imposing it certainly is, not only on account of its dimensions and style and crowded tables, but also on account of the quantum and variety one is expected to devour. For in succession we have shrimps and oysters, chicken, ham, roast beef, with surroundings of tomatoes, cranberry sauce, cabbage, turnip, boiled Indian corn, potatoes, bread, butter, &c., all of which are to be washed down with claret, or, if you are a teetotaller, with ice-water and tea. And such a dessert!—squash pie, custard pie, apple tart, ice-cream, with various sundries of cakes and fruit. Why the Americans are not all corpulent we are at loss to know, for certainly they are famous cooks and splendid feeders. But how they do it, in general, in such a *multum in parvo* style—that is, swallow so much in so short a time—is a problem not easy to be solved. Can it be that they swallow their meals as the whale swallowed Jonah ?—or how ?

And here, let me be permitted to say, nothing in this city, and indeed in American cities generally, impresses a stranger more than the number, the mag- nitude, and the elegance of the restaurants and hotels, in not a few of which entire American fami-

lies constantly live. The following extract from a
trustworthy source may give our readers some idea of
what we mean. "The city of hotels, New York
boasts about 108 of all sizes, and some of them of
enormous business. We do not know that any other
city in the world ever has had corresponding hotel
accommodation, and it is only the habits of the
Americans, and their readiness to live in hotels, that
at all explains the plentiful circumstances. Just
consider a few of the items which an enterprising
reporter of the *New York Tribune* has gathered from
the lips of the managers and proprietors of some of
the chief hotels. The figures astound and bewilder
one. We seem to be reading the calculations of a
mad gastronomer, when we turn to what they have to
say of the bullocks, the eggs, the oysters, the cans of
milk, the millions of fish annually consumed. Fifteen
hotels alone require 54,600 lbs. of fresh meat weekly.
Of this quantity about 35,000 lbs. are beef, and as a
bullock averages about 1,000 lbs. in weight, one
might perhaps suppose that a very few would suffice.
But consider that these hotels use, or profess to use,
only the best pieces, and it will be apparent that the
slaughter must be large indeed. The facts are that
about 330 bullocks every week, or 20,000 in the year,
are needed in order to fill the larders of these fifteen
hotels. 600,000 lbs. of fish and 15,000,000 bivalves
go the same hungry way ; 3,240 quarts of cream and
27,330 quarts of milk, 8,875 lbs. of butter, 13,210 lbs.
of sugar, 2,795 lbs. of coffee, and 685 lbs. of tea are
in the weekly bill of fare of these fifteen houses ; 5,290

head of game and 2,450 lbs. of poultry a week; 10,000 barrels of flour and 20,000 barrels of potatoes a year,—are among the articles consumed. One hotel uses four boxes of lemons a week in cooking; another uses a barrel of oranges in a day; and two or three of them have been known to consume weekly 3,000 lbs. of grapes. Of course, as members of the Anglo-Saxon race, our cousins like cleanliness, and soap is not with them what it is in the eyes of most Continental innkeepers—a luxury which only fastidious Englishmen ask for. The 15 hotels, which include the Grand Central, the St. Nicholas, the Sturtevant, the Windsor, and the Fifth Avenue Hotels, consume weekly 24,400 lbs. of soap. The washing of table linen, bed linen, towels, &c., signifies about 19,000,000 pieces in the year. The average weekly consumption of gas in these 15 gigantic establishments is 1,173,000 feet. They can provide, on an emergency, beds for 7,640 people, and they can comfortably accommodate 1,000 fewer. They support an army of 1,600 male servants, with as many females, and they boast of having 4,622 rooms; and it is estimated that the receipts of these 15 hotels average about £8,000 a day. We hope that these figures will soften travellers' hearts somewhat, and that they will not grumble so much as they do at the cost of putting up at a New York hotel. These edifices can be 'run' only at an enormous expense, and in connection with them waste, extravagance, and losses are inevitable. The very furniture lasts only five years, such is the wear and tear; and for half the year the greater

c

portion of the rooms may remain untenanted. Somebody must pay for all this, and if the receipts at certain seasons are immense, the outlay at all times is also on a vast scale. The hotel-keeper does not attempt to obtain what he imagines to be his due by charging exorbitant prices for indifferent wine, or encourage, we might even say demand and insist upon, its use. At the tables of the Grand Central, the Metropolitan, or the Windsor, wine is, in truth, little used, at least judging by English practice ; and if ever we can ' Americanize ' our dinner tables, as we have Americanized so many other institutions, our people will be more temperate than at present. But we have the statement of a proprietor of one of these large hotels, 'that the daily expenses were 2,500 dollars, while the receipts from the average daily number of guests, at five dollars per day, only amounted to 2,250 dollars,' thus showing a loss on the board bill of 250 dollars per day. 'This loss,' he says, 'has to be made up by *extras*, such as wine and cigars.' "

But it is an important question—how does this hotel and restaurant life affect the American people ? That it cannot contribute to their social comfort is, we think, certain. That these hotels and restaurants are useful, convenient, and comfortable in their way, who can doubt ? For to thousands of strangers, and to business people who cannot reach their homes, especially for the mid-day meal, they furnish ready and pleasant accommodation, and often, too, at a reasonable cost. Moreover, to those families that live in them they save a deal of trouble, in a community where servants are neither so cheap nor so abundant as they are with us.

But who that ever knew the quiet, cheerful comfort of an English home, with its plain but ample and palatable fare, its bright hearth, its laughing and frolicking little ones, its wisely and well-ordered subordination of children and servants, and its sacred seclusion from an obtruding and impertinent world—would willingly exchange it for a place of public resort, where meals are hastily swallowed at a common table, and where the amenities and sanctities of domestic life are of necessity almost unknown ?

Nor can such places, however orderly and carefully conducted, be friendly to the culture of religion and morals, especially those of young persons and females, who, in such circumstances, must of necessity see and hear what offends the moral sense. Besides, no family worship can, as a rule, be here ; no blessing asked upon the provided meal, no religious conversation—in fact, there can be none of the exercises that hallow and endear home, and that make the family circle a sacred training-ground for the Church and for heaven.

Upon many subsequent occasions, as well as upon this, such reflections have been strongly suggested to us, as, amid a crowd of strangers; with every possible personal and material comfort, we have eaten in social solitude our morning, mid-day, or evening meal.

CHAPTER III.

HERE, for the first time, our attention is specially drawn towards the Negro race. They are generally servants in hotels, restaurants, and private families; and in this capacity they seem remarkably quiet, orderly, and attentive; usually receiving their orders in silence, and executing them cheerfully, promptly, and with careful exactness. Of course, many of them are far from prepossessing in their features; but some are really good-looking, the majority stout and strong of limb, and all clean, neat, and, so far as they are able to assume it, showy in their dress.

What a libel on man, that any shallow-pated member of the Anthropological Society should tell us that these people are little better than monkeys! Here is one—a genuine darky, thick-lipped, broad nosed, high-cheeked, woolly-headed. Born in the West Indies, he is now professor in a college in Liberia. We are looking at him and listening to him with admiration, as, with graceful and modest gesture, and in well-chosen and carefully-accented English, he is, by cogent argument and the logic of well-arranged facts, inciting an assembly of Christian ministers to missionary zeal and effort in behalf of his neglected race. Is this not a man and a brother? Yes, and

he is somewhat of a wit too ; for, having been asked
by one of his audience, "What about the morality of
these African tribes of which you speak : are they
honest ?" He replies with an assumption of *naïveté*,
which we have seldom seen surpassed, "Yes, more
honest than you are here ; for I have traversed
hundreds of miles of their country without losing anything : but, yesterday, as I travelled in one of your
street-cars, I was relieved of my purse containing
sixty dollars." This reply elicited considerable merriment, at a time when banks, trust companies, and
mercantile firms were "bursting up" in all directions;
and when stock-holders and others, who a little before
had figured among the "big-bugs" of the City, and
made "a great splurge" in society, were reported to
be left without a cent. Nor was this wit of our sable
friend without profit ; for, then and there, a subscrip-
tion was made, that almost entirely recuperated him
for his loss. Of these interesting people there are
five millions in the States, most of whom—thanks to
the *quondam* slave lords—are totally untutored ; and
though the Church organizations, especially those of
the Methodists and Baptists, together with the Freed-
man's Aid and other philanthropic societies, are
doing much to improve their condition, yet how their
religious and educational necessities can be adequately met, is a question more easily asked than
answered.

For the lower order of Irish—especially since the
notable doings of Bill T—— and Company—the New
Yorker has a supreme contempt ; and often amuses

himself and his company with anecdotes of Paddy's romantic hopes, political proclivities, and wit.

For example, we were told with a grim, dry, half-malicious humour, of a certain member of the Hibernian community who, having landed at Castle Gardens, observed a dollar lying on the ground. Pat eyed it for a moment; and then, with a look and in a tone of undisguised scorn, addressed it thus,—"Arrah, do ye think I'd be bothered picking *you* up? I'll go up here above, and shovel thim up by the thousand."

Another, having been asked by a zealous Yankee canvasser to vote for a certain political party, declared he knew nothing about their parties and was indifferent as to whom he should vote for. The persistent Yankee pressed his request; but found it impossible to make his Irish friend apprehend the difference between Republican and Democrat. At length, almost despairing of success, he asked: "Will you vote *for* the Government or *against* it?" To which the honest Hibernian replied with indignant warmth, "Why, to be sure, *against* it."

We were also favoured with the following by a gentleman who had been across the Atlantic, visited Cork, and hired a *gingleman* to drive him to Blarney. The journey over and the fare paid, this worthy representative of charioteering Phaeton shrugged his shoulders, and asked for something additional as a gratuity for himself. Our American friend handed him a sixpence; which Pat, instead of putting in his pocket, held and significantly eyed in the open palm of his hand. Then, looking in the face of the stranger, he said in a tone of well-affected pathos : "Dear me ! that American war was an awful thing." "Why so?" inquired the other. "Because," replies Pat, "it kilt off all the shilling men, and left none but the sixpenny men alive."

We are much struck with the magnitude, elegance, and comfort of many of, the "stores" or business houses in New York. Of course, Stewart's retail establishment in Broadway could not fail to attract our notice. It is built of cast iron, highly ornamented, and painted beautifully white. It is, in fact, an imitation of Grecian architecture in snowy marble ; with a double front, one in Broadway, and another in Fourth Avenue ; and covering the area of an entire block. It is, if we recollect aright, five stories high, and looks a vast and harmonious mass of pilasters, arched windows, mouldings, and cornices. Within, it is as beautiful as without ; being everywhere pure white, and covered with chaste and elaborate ornament,—such as imitations of leaves, fruit, flowers, &c. —in bold and handsome relief. Mirrors, glass-cases filled with costly fabrics, and long-extending counters are everywhere to be seen ; while rows of velvet-covered seats, fixed on pivots, and resembling piano stools, run all along in front of the counters, for the purpose of accommodating customers while purchasing their goods. The floors are in many places covered with costly carpet ; and the warerooms are throughout provided with hot-air pipes ; so that when the glass street-doors are closed in winter, which they always are, nobody in the establishment suffers anything from cold winds and biting frosts.

Many other houses approach Stewart's in size and style; and it is pleasant in all of them, and indeed, in the business establishments everywhere, to observe that, when genial autumn has given place to the rigours of winter, the arrangements for heating are so complete that none of the people doing business behind the counter or at the desk is to be seen looking white and blue in the face, blowing his aching sausage-shaped fingers for the purpose of soothing half-broken chilblains, and moving, like a soldier marking time on parade, to prevent the sluggish blood from freezing in his toes.

Indeed, it strikes us that in household arrangement, convenience, and comfort, the mass of the American people excel us much. Their system of heating, by furnaces from below and stoves above, though, in general, yielding too high a temperature, which we think is one reason why American women and children look so pale as they do, is really admirable; warming alike parlours, hall, dormitories, in fact, all places from the basement to the attics, and saving one, when in doors, from the disagreeable alternative of being obliged either to wear inconveniently heavy garments or to shiver with cold.

Perhaps it may not be amiss to give some idea of what American houses generally are—how they look, and of what they consist. A very few words will tell. The highest class are of brown stone, lofty and mansion-looking, and fenced in front with iron railings. The hall guarded by two doors—the outer of which is solid and handsome, and stands always open; and the inner, with large glass panels covered inside with blinds, is always closed—is generally approached from the street by a flight of ascending steps that are fenced on either side with an ornamental balustrade. A silver-plated bell-pull supersedes every kind of knocking apparatus. The windows, all of which are furnished with Venetian blinds, open upon commodious verandahs; many of which in summer are covered with awnings, and afford a refreshing retreat at eventide from the sultry and oppressive atmosphere within. The basement, lofty, well lighted, well heated in winter, and cool in summer, and well furnished, contains dining-room, kitchen behind, and other cognate domiciliary apartments. Immediately above, and on a level with the hall, are the parlours or reception-rooms and the library; and, as a rule, though there are a good many exceptions, all higher stories are dedicated to the needful relaxation of somniferous repose.

Domiciles graduating downward through brick to wood, are all built and arranged on the same general plan; only, of course, the size, beauty, and costliness of their furniture are on a diminishing scale, until the point is reached which combines inexpensive simplicity with neatness and comfort.

That there are numbers of houses in such cities as New York, once inhabited by the wealthy, but now crowded with dirty tenement lodgers, is not to be wondered at; since the improvident, the intemperate,

the vicious, and the poor are ever thronging to the
great centres of population and commerce; yet,
the number of this class is incomparably less than
the multitudes of ragged, half-starved, and shiftless
people stowed away in the lanes, alleys, and dilapi-
dated suburbs of European cities and great manufac-
turing towns. But here is an inside glimpse of one
of the best houses in New York.

We are kindly invited to a reception to be given by
the Honourable Mr. G.; so let us go. At 8 p.m.,
we reach the house of our hospitable friend, and, in
answer to the summons of the bell, the door is opened
by a portly darky in black suit and white gloves,
whose broad ebony face is unctuous with politeness
and good nature. Up a broad, handsome staircase,
we are ushered to the luxuriously furnished dressing-
rooms, where we deposit hat and overcoat; and
having adjusted our toilet, we descend to the reception-rooms, at the entrance of which we are politely
taken by the arm by a gentleman who introduces us
to the Honourable Mr. and Mrs. G. Of course we
make our bow, and are most kindly received; and
after an interchange of a few commonplace civilities,
we mingle with the crowd who throng a suite of
spacious and lofty apartments connected by folding-
doors that stand wide open to receive an unusual
number of guests.

Such costly furniture, decorations, pictures, books,
and ornaments as might be expected in a fine house
are all present; music is sweetly fiddled by professional minstrels, stowed away in an alcove at the

extremity of the inmost apartment, and numerous jets shed a brilliant light on jewelled ladies and care-fully-dressed gentlemen, who either sit, stand, lounge, saunter, or promenade at will.

In an adjoining apartment refreshments—stewed oysters, salmon, ice-cream, iced coffee, fruits, and sweetmeats—are partaken of in the usual American way, standing ; and a little before midnight, after a few splendidly dull hours, we slip off, with the irrepressible conviction that the Church (for this was a gathering of Christians) is in many of its features not very unlike the world, and that Republican plain-ness may sometimes tread closely upon the heels of old-country aristocratic display.

Yet, let no one suppose that Christianity is not in earnest in America, or that its people are not cordially attached to republican institutions. The American mind is essentially democratic, and so great is the freedom of opinion and action allowed, both by law and by conventional usage, that one might well doubt whether lawless licentiousness might not overturn the foundations of society in the great Republic, but for the conserving and salutary influences exerted by living and aggressive churches. But of this we shall have occasion to say more again.

Sometimes as we stroll along the streets, looking into newsvendors' stalls, and reading the great staring placards that are to be met with at every corner, we cannot help exclaiming—what a curse to the youth of this land must be the theatre and the sensational novel ! Whether the theatre here is worse than it is

in the Old Country we find it impossible to say, for
we are practically unacquainted with both ; but, if
one might judge from the showy placards that everywhere meet the gaze in New York, there is no species
of treachery, violence, and libertine blackguardism
that is not picturesquely represented on its theatrical
stage. Many of the illustrated newspapers, and externally ornamented novels hold forth to the public
eye, in the by-ways and thoroughfares, the same
examples of vice, and one is tempted to think that the
moral sentiment of a professedly Christian people
must be far below what it should be, who, with the
powers of government in their own hands, do not
repress and indignantly annihilate so tremendous a
mode of thrusting images of odious, yet seductive,
wickedness before the minds of the young. In view
of what is to be seen in some great cities of the Old
Country, it may indeed be retorted *et tu quoque.* But
we doubt if this is quite true ; so far as it is true, we
deplore it ; and we as heartily denounce public apathy
in reference to such demoralising street-exhibitions,
so far as they exist, in Great Britain, as we do the
public indifference that tolerates them here.

One day, as we approach City Hall, our attention is
attracted by unusual excitement : what can it mean ?
Men are standing in groups,—some gaping with
wonder ; some talking, laughing, and shaking hands ;
and some, halting in front of a monster placard, are
eagerly reading words that are written in large and
legible letters. It is headed—"JUSTICE TRIUMPHANT!"
Why this is strange ! Is not justice always

triumphant in this great, intelligent, highly-civilized, and self-governing community? Not so. Justice here is not quite so blind as her symbolical representations declare her to be ; but, with at least one eye open, she too often inclines the scale to the side that presents her with the heaviest bribe. And so now, because a great city official, who, with his *confrères*, has committed enormous public frauds, has been convicted of swindling and sentenced to penal servitude for a term of years, the people seem filled with astonishment and almost frantic with joy. Surely the security and happiness of a people are very much less dependent upon systems and forms of government, however important in themselves, than upon the honour and integrity of the persons by whom they are administered. Such are our thoughts, as we turn again away from City Hall and its excited crowds, and again mingle with the living stream that passes along the side-walks of Broadway.

Subsequently, conversing with a friend who has spent almost the entire of a long life in America, who has filled important public offices, and who well knows and loves the country, its institutions, and its people, he remarks : ''The theory of our Government is beautiful ; but I am persuaded it is the most corruptly administered that the world has ever yet seen.'' Language so strong, a condemnation so sweeping, spoken without passion or excitement, and coming from the lips of a man of high intelligence, unquestionable veracity, and strong Republican politics, is startling to hear. Indeed we are disposed to think, without at all doubting the sincerity of the speaker, they must be received *cum grano salis;* and yet we not very long after hear from no less a man than the eloquent and patriotic Talmage that—"Bribery is one of the most appalling sins of this country."

Surely, this state of things cannot last among a community so enlightened and so largely permeated with the principles of the Christian religion. Either the form of government must be changed, which it is not likely to be ; or the nation must indignantly arise, and, in the greatness of its might, shake off and crush the viperous broods of speculating politicians, who, under the hypocritical pretence of patriotic zeal, are seeking place and emolument, while they poison the fountains of legislation and judgment, and voraciously suck away the moral vitality of a victimised people. Of course, these remarks do not apply to all American politicians, much less to her leading statesmen ; but if we can believe what we continually hear among the people, as well as what we read in the daily newspaper press, they must apply to too many.

In New York one soon gets accustomed to that peculiar nasal mode of uttering our language for which Americans are noted ; and what at first sounds so unpleasant, soon becomes ordinary and familiar, and ceases to offend the ear. That this nasal music is an excrescence many well-educated Americans frankly admit. But they deny that it is American ; and regard it as an exotic accomplishment, imported from Old England by their Puritan ancestors, and left with other similarly valuable

English bequests, as a linguistic inheritance to themselves. On this head, let us listen to one of our intelligent and cultured cousins beyond:—" 'Tis true that many Americans are exceedingly careless in their speech. They do talk through their noses ; but it is also true that this dreadful habit is an English inheritance, and is not due to climate. The native American's voice is guttural. Our pilgrim fathers brought over the whine known in England as 'Suffolk singing,' which though banished from London *salons*, may be heard in the counties of Norfolk, Suffolk, Essex, and Cambridge. If our ancestors, who named Massachusetts counties after their old homes, had had good ears for music, they would have left their noses behind them, and their descendants would not now be twanging through life. Nasality has so permeated the atmosphere of New England, that its people do not realise the affront they put upon their vocal organs. Yet, in spite of hereditary taint, the most musical English in the world is spoken by cultivated Bostonians." And again,—"The Puritans, however, are not alone to blame for our defects of speech. Africa has been our bane in more than one respect, and Southerners drawl and flatten their vowels because their sable nurses did so before them. Nevertheless, the cultured Southern planter will often speak English without the slightest accent. Puritan and Negro have spread over the Continent their vocal peculiarities, and until all parents appreciate that most excellent thing in man or woman, a sonorous voice, Americans will suffer under the imputation of being the worst toned of people." Such we learn are some of the advantages conferred on Columbia by the joint influence of Britisher and Negro. How far this is true, it is not our province to judge. We prefer allowing the Americans, the English, and the Negroes to settle the matter among themselves.

CHAPTER IV.

But come, let us look at the churches. These are numerous. They belong to different denominations, are of all sizes and styles, and are externally not very different from those with which we are familiar at home. And so, without staying to note and criticise architectural proportions and structure, let us cross Broadway, and visit a church in which divine service is about to be held.

The building is a good one, in plain Grecian style, and approached by a not very lofty flight of brown stone steps. Below is the usual American basement, with committee-rooms, vestry, and large apartment in which the Sunday-school is just now being held. About 300 children are present, with the customary proportion of teachers and other officials ; and everything is going on in the ordinary way. But as it is near the time of closing, a hymn is sung, accompanied by a harmonium, such as every American school is furnished with ; and then the children are conducted to the church above. This is the "audience room," a parallelogram capable of holding eight or nine hundred people, with galleries on three sides, and—as all American churches are—well lighted, well ventilated, well heated, well carpeted, furnished with

D

comfortably upholstered seats, and provided with a platform instead of a pulpit.

By the way, of this platform rostrum in the American churches we have heard a good deal; and we have heard pulpit reformers in the Old Country say,—"Away with the old tub, and up with the American platform instead." But now we are convinced that many of these vociferous ecclesiastical levellers scarcely understand what they are shouting for. The American platform is admirable for convenience, comfort, appearance, and even effect; but to knock down the old pulpit in many, indeed in most, of our galleried churches, and replace it by a platform, would be to put the minister, when officiating, in the position of Jack before he jumps up in the box.

The truth is, in America, the whole building—in its width, the size and angle of its galleries, and even the elevation of its floor—is adjusted to the platform; whereas, in most of our churches, in consequence of their proportions and internal arrangements, no such adjustment can possibly be. It is true that the altitude of some of our ministerial elevators might with advantage be a good deal reduced; but to abolish them *in toto*, would be not to improve, but to mar, and to hide from the eyes of the people the man who ministers to them the Word. But to return.

The service begins by the giving out and singing of a hymn, the music of which is harmoniously rendered by the whole congregation led by a middling choir, which is assisted by an organ. A short portion of Scripture is

read by the minister alone ; for no one else opens a
Bible, nor, indeed, do there appear any Bibles to be
opened. An extemporaneous prayer follows—brief
and hurried enough, and not followed by the Lord's
Prayer or any other formula except a final Amen.
Another hymn, well and generally sung, follows ;
announcements are made, and the text is given out.
Then comes a sermon, partly read, partly extemporised, hurriedly uttered, and singularly free from
theological stamina, Scriptural exegesis and quota-
tion, pathos, and incisive power. Then follows a
mode of making a collection, quite usual, we are told,
among all denominations in America, but to us
singularly queer. The affair is as follows :—

Minister : "You know we are to have our Sunday-school collection to-day. So you must give
liberally. Want two hundred dollars. Can't do with
less. Brethren, take your pencils. Go round. Brother
A——, take this side. Brother S——, take that
side. Brother W——, take the centre. Now
brethren, begin. Quick! Who will give five dollars ?
Who will give three dollars ? Who will give a dollar ?
Now, brethren, quick! quick!"

A Voice : "I'll give five dollars."

Minister : "Very good. Put it down. Now,
brethren, quick !"

Another Voice : "I'll give five dollars."

Another Voice : "I'll give three dollars."

Minister : "Very good. Put down Mr. T——
three dollars. That's right." (Rubbing his hands
and smiling.) "Now, brethren, quick—quick !

Give your names. Must be done. We'll soon have it."

And so this process goes on for about a quarter of an hour; voices, sometimes in an undertone and sometimes quite loud, announcing sundry donations from one dollar up to ten; the brethren putting down and collecting; and the minister rubbing his hands, smiling, and ejaculating, at becoming intervals, notes of encouragement and praise. At length there is a pause.

Minister: "Well, brethren, have you got it? See, reckon. Just let's see how much you have."

Brethren (having entered and totted): "We have a hundred and twenty dollars."

Minister: "Then, want just eighty dollars more. Now, brethren, go round again. Must get this eighty dollars. Can't do without it. Money wanting for school. Quick, brethren. Who'll make up the eighty dollars? Who'll help? I'll give another dollar myself. Yes, I will. Now, brethren, quick!"

A Voice: "I'll give ten dollars more."

Minister: "Good, good! That's right. Now go on."

Other voices announce further donations, and a long pause ensues; the people, meanwhile, looking interested and good-humoured.

Minister: "Now, brethren, count."

Brethren count, and sixty additional dollars are announced.

Minister: "Good! we have now a hundred and eighty dollars. Want *just* twenty more. *Only* twenty more. Go round again, brethren. *Must* get the other twenty. Can't do without the twenty dollars."

The people are silent. They look at each other; they smile; they nod; they seem a little fidgety.

Minister: "Well, this won't do. MUST get. the other twenty."

A Voice: "I'll give five."

Another Voice: "I'll give three more."

Minister: "*Good!* we'll soon have it. *Eight* of the twenty already. Go on, brethren. *Only* TWELVE more wanting. Quick, brethren; quick!"

At length the brethren announce that the entire sum is made up; and the people, evidently pleased that the two hundred dollars are forthcoming for the Sunday-school, and that the boring process is concluded, smile at each other, and shrug their shoulders as if they thought it full time to go. But, not yet.

Minister, rubbing his hands and radiant with complacent smiles, "Excellent, indeed! We'll get along *now*. That'll do. The *trustees* will now take the baskets, and go round, and take up *their usual* collection." The trustees go round with small white baskets, and receive the collection. The doxology is sung, the benediction pronounced, and the congregation dismissed.

To us a great deal of what we have witnessed seems painfully irreverent, and even comical—unbecoming the place, unbecoming the day, and unbecoming the occasion; but this, mayhap, is only Old Country prejudice, the offspring of a narrow conventionalism which the world is rapidly outgrowing, and with which the advocates of an offhand progress can have no sympathy whatever. Well, be it so. Yet we shall continue to stick to the old-fashioned notions, that the unstinted and reverent reading of God's Word is an important part of public worship ; that sermons ought to be extemporaneous, expository, and strengthened with a good theological backbone ; that public extemporaneous prayer at the opening of a service is none the worse for having the Lord's Prayer added to it ; and that a minister on the Lord's day, even when appealing for a collection in behalf of some religious and benevolent object, ought not so much as to seem to imitate the grotesque antics of an adroit auctioneer.

But let us in justice say that subsequent experience has taught us that, though there is too little reading of the Word of God in American churches, and too little exegesis of Scripture and dogmatic theology in their pulpits, and too much auctioneering about their public collections, yet very often their religious assemblies are pervaded by a spirit of earnest and even fervid devotion, and not unfrequently from the pulpits is sounded forth the old Gospel in tones of alternate thunder and melting love.

But the American prayer-meeting, ordinarily held twice a week, and, at special seasons, every night for weeks in succession, is really admirable, and a great source of strength and increase to the churches. This meeting is usually held in the school-room, and is well attended. The pastor presides, surrounded by a number of prayer-leaders, each of whom is at liberty to commence a hymn or to lead in prayer as he feels disposed, and as opportunity offers ; so that the meeting is really not so much the minister's as the people's ; and it is usually sustained with great spirit during an hour and a half, and sometimes for even a longer period. Often, too, it is turned into a meeting for the relation of religious experience ; and many brief, pointed, and soul-stirring testimonies are borne to the mercy and grace of God, and to the reality and power of experimental religion ; while thoughtless persons are exhorted to seriousness, and penitents are encouraged to trust, then and there, in Christ as their Saviour.

Usually each church has its "protracted meeting" during the winter—which means, a succession of prayer-meetings, night after night, during six or eight weeks—when it expects to have its own religious life quickened, and to make aggression on the world outside. It is true, this has been sometimes abused, like almost every other good thing, leading people to rely too much on impulse and feeling, and prompting to spasmodic effort to "get up" a revival ; yet after an observation of these meetings during many months, and in different parts of the widely-extended continent, we cannot resist the conclusion that to them, more than to pulpit ministrations (though the importance of these cannot be overrated), is mainly due the rapid growth of the American churches.

Indeed, after much observation, the conclusion is forced upon us that, notwithstanding many powerful and splendid exceptions, America is weak in her pulpit, but wonderfully strong in her organizations for prayer. And surely we must admit that there is real power here ; if we believe, as we are bound to believe, that living Christianity is the work of God's Spirit, and that the Spirit is given in answer to prayer.

Rich, varied, and abundant is the supply of fruit in this favoured land ; and as we are invited by a friend to a "Fruit Festival," let us step into a street-car and go. This is a commodious vehicle, but often inconveniently crowded. The seats are comfortable, though one had better not look at the floor, which bears unsightly marks of the too general habit of spitting. One gentleman opposite us,—with scrupulously neat turned-down shirt-collar, and with wide-expanding vest, from which glares forth a snowy linen front sparkling with golden studs—after looking thoughtfully for some time, as if his brain was in a state of painful incubation, opens his grave jaws; when out flaps, with splashing sound, what appears the yolk of an egg, but what is in reality a well-chewed quid, with its black nucleus and its ample surroundings of supernumerary saliva. O my stomach ! How art thou disquieted ; and with what instinctive rapidity do our feet retreat before the unclean inundation, lest our boots should be unfitted to appear at the festival of fruit.

But we have got to the place,—the school-room of a church which is yet to be built, but for which an ample site has been procured by zealous trustees. And what a school-room !—so large, so commodious, so beautiful, so splendidly lit, and so conveniently, handsomely, and even luxuriously furnished. Ample tables are groaning beneath a weight of fruits, flowers, confectionery, and ice-cream ; while hundreds of elegantly-dressed, intelligent, bright-eyed children are laughingly and wistfully peering at the delicious feast of which they are presently to partake.

Grace is sung, the feast begins; and straightway apples, pears, strawberries, ice-cream, and cakes are in rapid circulation, and are hastily disappearing through the open mouths of a multitude of little sunny-faced children. The big people too,—for many adults are present,—seem nothing loath to mingle in the fray, and to aid in disburthening the tables of their abundant and delicious provisions. But when all are amply satisfied, there is still as much left as would furnish another similar feast, and leave a margin over. Then, fruit, big cakes, bouquets, and such-like are auctioned amid much innocent mirth, and the proceeds of the sales aid in defraying the cost of the feast.

Of course, addresses follow; the most remarkable of which is made by an American, who is introduced as ''Brother M——, who has just returned after doing Europe.'' .And what a woeful description of Europe follows! Never have our ears heard of anything so much in need of American compassion as poor, unhappy, half-starved Europe. Brother M—— had been in Switzerland, and could see nothing there but the poverty of the peasantry. No places or monuments of historic interest, no picturesque beauty, no

institutions of learning or of political freedom, seem
to have come within the range of his cultured vision.
He had been in England, and could get nothing eat-
able there—not an apple, a pear, nor, alas! "*even
a dough-nut.*" Even in London itself, *mirabile
dictu!* he could not obtain a bit of tolerable plum-
pudding. In fact, the mortification of this gentleman's American stomach during his European tour is
the great burthen of his pitiful harangue; and the
drift of the whole is to make the impression on the
minds of these children that no good thing can come
out of Europe, and that their own America must be
the very Paradise of terrestrial creation. Is it any
wonder that with such instructors as Brother M——,
who, by the way, is not a minister, but a highly
intelligent layman, many juvenile Americans should
grow up with mistaken views of other people and
other lands, and that their minds should be crammed
to the full with the most blinding prejudice and the
most laughable conceit?

But before taking our leave of the festival of fruit
—which, on the whole, we greatly admired and
enjoyed—let us say a word or two about American
ministerial garb.

The worthy pastor of this church was present—we
believe a genuine American; and, as Americans
generally are, exceedingly agreeable, courteous, and
bland. But how unclerical-looking to European eyes!
There he is—a neat, trim, dapper, well-shaven,
shining-faced man, with whiskers as symmetrically
cut, and as carefully combed as those of some of our

clerical dandies at home. Beneath his long-peaked, turned-down shirt-collar is a black neckerchief tied in a sailor's knot, under which is a broad shirt-front, on which is a snowy vest surmounted by the wide lapels of a most carefully-tailored swallow-tailed coat. Whether he wore a white hat we don't know, nor can we now say whether his pants were black, lavender, or brown ; nor can we positively affirm, for we did not see them, whether his gloves were yellow or green. But certain we are that American ministers as a rule,—though many of them dress plainly enough, —do not feel themselves bound, by any regard for gravity of appearance or by any conventional rules, to adopt garments of any special colour or cut. Indeed, the black tie, white vest, and, in summer, white hat are common ; and with these we have sometimes seen green gloves, coloured pants, and a snuff-colour coat of the ordinary style. The fact is, in general, ministers are not recognised by their dress in America. Whether they should be or not is, perhaps, a mere matter of taste; yet we are inclined to think that, while in his dress the minister of the Gospel should neither be aspiring to the priest nor exhibiting the clerical buck, his garments should fairly harmonise with the nature and gravity of his work.

Then, we will not affirm that the most becoming way of introducing a minister to a miscellaneous religious meeting or social gathering is by the fraternal and familiar appellation—brother. Very much amused we were indeed, when, on one occasion, we heard a Sunday-school superintendent introduce

an elderly minister to a number of very junior
scholars as "The Reverend brother S——." And
when, on another occasion, we saw a slim-looking
lady run up to a venerable bishop of corpulent outline
and weighty proportions, shake him by the hand, and
exclaim, "O, how do you do, brother K——?" we
could hardly keep from laughing outright. Subsequently the lady took the bishop to several of her
acquaintances who were present, in each case introducing him by saying, "This is brother K——."
We are not sure that even in times of apostolic
simplicity ministers of the Gospel were thus familiarly
brothered by all the men, women, and children who
. happened to come into the church.

We have spoken of the want of theological
backbone in too many American sermons ; from
which some might infer that the study of Scripture
exegesis, homiletics, and systematic theology, is
neglected in this country. We should be sorry to
make any such impression ; for seminaries and
colleges that give instruction in these branches are
to be found all over the land, are well sustained,
and give unmistakable signs of increasing efficiency
and worth.

Amongst others, we visited Drew Theological
Seminary, belonging to the Methodist Episcopal
Church, and founded by the munificent liberality of
Samuel Drew, Esq., one of the merchant princes of
New York. It is situated near Madison, a beautiful
village of New Jersey, and commands a wide view of
a picturesque and exquisitely beautiful country. The

Seminary buildings, with professors' houses detached, are surrounded by a shady and ornamental park of ninety-five acres, and accommodate a large number of students who are in careful training for efficient ministerial work. It has the nucleus of a good library ; and, with a superior staff of professors, it affords to the student every facility for cultivating the highest branches of literature and of theological science. Pleasant and grateful are our recollections of the bright, beautiful, and socially happy day spent by us at this abode sacred to the highest of all sciences, and of the gentlemanly courtesy and genial hospitality shown us by the principal members of the faculty.

But how is it that, with such institutions and such appreciation in high quarters of biblical and theological studies, so many of the sermons to which we have listened have been so poor in the muscle and vigour that wield with masculine energy the sword of the Spirit, so as to convince men of sin and to lead them to God ? Can it be that, amongst a people too many of whom are morbidly fond of sensation, there is a greater desire on the part of the preacher to please than to profit ; and that *conscience* is left untouched, lest it should diminish the attendance in the pews, and give trustees and other church officials . occasion to say,—"Our collections are smaller, and we must have a more popular man ? "

Yet, in this land of popular sermons, as well as popular everything else, we have occasionally listened to discourses of great intelligence, of great plainness, and of great power. In St. Paul's Methodist Episcopal Church, a handsome Gothic structure in one of the principal avenues of the city, and indeed in many other places, not only in New York, but in other parts of the country, we have with pleasure and, we trust, also with profit, listened to discourses which, for clear and full exposition, good sense, apt and striking illustration, and stirring appeal, have been all that one could wish.

But what would some of our Old Country folk think of such a passage in a sermon as this, which was reported as having been delivered by a popular preacher in Brooklyn, during our stay in New York? After a vivid and appalling description of the place of torment, and of the woeful doom of the lost, the preacher went on to say: "*I* know *some* that are in hell! And *you* know them too. They have occupied *these* pews. Would you like to hear who they are?" —Here the people, wondering and staring, and almost overcome with horror, are scarcely able to breathe. The preacher continues: "Well, I will tell you. They are the *fathers* and *mothers* of some of *yourselves!*" What the effect was, our readers can judge. Next day we read in the New York press a scathing and well-merited rebuke of this horrible attempt at being sensational in the pulpit, and of so outrageous and ghastly an effort to terrify people out of their sins.

"The Preachers' Meeting," consisting of the city ministers and other ministers belonging to the Methodist Episcopal Church, and held every Monday morning in the rooms of the Methodist Book Concern, is an assembly of considerable importance ; occupying its sitting one Monday in the month with purely devotional exercises, and the other three Mondays with the discussion of ecclesiastical and other matters, especially those connected with the Methodist Episcopal Church. Papers are read on church-membership, Sunday-schools, temperance, and other kindred subjects ; and these often give rise to discussions that are able, lively, and conducted in the best possible spirit. The meetings are attended by about a hundred ministers, are sometimes addressed by laymen, and are always, as almost all gatherings in America are, open to the public.

As it is Monday morning, and as the brethren are gathering, we may as well go in. Up we mount long flights of steeply-ascending stairs, till, a little bit puffed, we reach the lobbies, and enter the room where a goodly number are already assembled, waiting for the proceedings to begin. The broad, square, lofty apartment is comfortably carpeted and seated, and its walls are hung with portraits in oil of some of the most notable and venerable ministers of the church. Elder E—— is presiding ; and at his right hand is the secretary, who aids in conducting the business of the meeting, and records its transactions.

A hymn is sung with lusty voice and hearty goodwill, a portion of Scripture read, and prayer offered up with glowing and refreshing fervour. Reading the minutes by the secretary follows ; and then a

paper is read by one of the ministers present, on
"The Argument from Design," in proof of the
existence of God. Strangely enough, as we think,
the writer considers, and attempts to show, that this
argument is inconclusive and nugatory. But the
paper elicits little discussion ; as, in the estimation
of those present, the position of the writer is absurd,
and his reasoning unworthy of serious refutation.
After devotional exercises, the meeting adjourns.

To the same place we repair in the afternoon of
another day, to hear a lecture on elocution, chiefly
intended for the benefit of ministers. As the lecture
proceeds, such grammar, such nasal melody, such
affected and meaningless gesticulation, such inane
straining after effect are exhibited to our ears and
eyes, as make the whole affair a rare treat for our
wondering curiosity. But are we dreaming ?—as we
listen to the barefaced effrontery that recommends to
a number of Christian ministers the theatre, or the
opera-house, as a fit and profitable school where they
may receive lessons in elocution. And yet we are
astonished that, at the close of this layman's marvellous lecture to the clergy, nobody expresses the
slightest dissent. That dissent is felt we cannot
but believe ; but surely no sense of fastidious and
morbid propriety, or feeling of delicate reserve in the
minds of his auditors, should allow so presumptuous
and impudent a charlatan to take his departure
"unwhipped." Yet unwhipped he departs ; taking
with him, too, as the reward of his literary and
oratorical toil, a goodly number of dollars and cents.

Indeed, we are of opinion that of the many humbugs tolerated by the good nature of the American people, the professional lecturer is often, *par excellence*, the greatest of all. He is not, perhaps, so mischievous as the stumping politician, who goes his rounds vending party slang, and blowing up the flames of popular wrath ; but he is, if possible, a more pretentious, self-inflated, and ridiculous sham.

CHAPTER V.

To the West. Though not to the "Far West;" for our destination is South Bend, Indiana, about eight hundred miles from New York. A short time ago, this would have seemed a long and formidable journey; but now that we are in America, where almost everything is on so large a scale, and where the means of locomotion are so ample and facile, it seems commonplace enough. So, without any special concern about the length of the way, we prepare to set out.

A ticket, or rather a series of tickets all printed on the same slip, is obtained at an office in Broadway, together with "checks" for our baggage. We say for our baggage, for the word *luggage* is not used by our cousins beyond. And now we are, for the first time, sensibly impressed with the difference between railway travelling in America and railway travelling at home. At home one must drive to the railway-station, must get his luggage left on the platform, must wait until it is the pleasure of the clerk to open the ticket-office — must, within a few minutes of the starting-time, at the risk of bruised hat, torn coat-skirts, and trampled corns, elbow his way through an anxious crowd, all of whom are crushing forward to the insignificant and half-barricaded

counter, behind which stands the stately and indifferent official who hands out the tickets and takes in the
cash,—must crush his way out of the crowd, rush
back to the platform, look for his luggage, get it
labelled and put in the van—must, if he have them
with him, rush off and look for his wife and children ;
and, just as the bell is ringing, must cram himself,
puffing and blowing, into almost any seat he can find,
lest, after all his forethought, punctuality, and care,
the guard should slam the door of the carriage, blow
his whistle, and leave him behind.

The American plan is better. It excludes all this
annoyance, fuss, and bluster ; for, now that we have
our ticket and checks, we know that, without interference on our part, our luggage will be punctually
and safely forwarded to its destination ; and we ourselves can go to the railway-station, or depot, quietly
and leisurely, and, without any confusion, select for
ourselves such a seat as we may think proper to
choose. And so we do.

Our route is by the Erie line. We therefore
cross to Jersey City in a steam-propelled ferryboat,
with comfortable cabins along the deck at each side,
crammed in the centre with horses and wagons, and
pyramidal piles of goods, and carrying a dense crowd
of passengers of all classes and of every age and sex.
We are soon in the depot. We say the *depot;* for
Americans never talk of a *terminus,* or of a *railway-
station.* The "cars"—not *carriages,* as we say—
are of immense size ; and are entered, not by a low
door at the side, but by a commodious door at the

end,—a door that is approached by a platform attached
to the car, and which platform is ascended by two or
three steps at either side, and carefully guarded by a
strong iron rail.

And, now that we are in, how convenient, comfortable, and even elegant everything seems. At each
end is a mirror, a closet, a large ornamental vessel
filled with iced water, and an immense stove. The
roof is lofty, airy, and handsome. The seats, in two
long parallel rows, are separated by an ample passage
in the centre, with velvet cushions, comfortably
upholstered reclining backs, and convenient foot-
boards in front. The floor is richly carpeted. In
fact everything is present that can make travelling a
luxury, and all is for the poor man as well as for the
rich. Were it not for the vile and disagreeably suggestive spittoon, the whole surroundings are calculated
to please; but, we confess, the appearance of this
ugly American necessity in some measure abates the
enjoyment we feel. Suddenly, a voice outside—not
the voice of the *guard*, but of the "conductor"—cries,
in imperative tones,—"All aboard!" and in a moment or two, without any premonitory sound of whistle
or bell, our long and well-filled train is moving ahead.

It is evening. The star of day has already dipped
below the horizon, and deepening shadows admonish
us of the speedy advent of approaching night. A
sleeping-car is attached; but, with plenty of muffling
and a roomy and well-cushioned seat, we prefer saving
our dollars, and staying where we are. Soon everything without is lost to view; and nothing is seen

save the car within, its living freight, and its not very brilliant lights. Our fellow-travellers are all well-dressed, common-sense people ; and most of them, either wearied and listless, or naturally taciturn, seem indisposed to talk.

On we go, at a rather slower rate than we used to do in the Old Country, gliding through several small towns or suburban villages, which are visible only by their street lamps, and by the lights that glimmer in the windows of their shops. Of course, we stop for a short time in the usual way; and at the stopping-places passengers drop out, and others come in. And in this journey, as well as in many subsequent ones, we are struck with the fact that this dropping out and coming in is continued almost the entire night ; indicating that the Americans are great travellers, using their locomotives almost as much by night as they do by day.

At length, we pull up at a station with a good restaurant, and supper is announced. A general rush follows ; and presently we are comfortably seated in a brilliantly-lit apartment, at a table amply furnished with tea, coffee, chicken, ham, hot beef-steaks, potatoes, mashed turnips, boiled Indian corn, together with miscellaneous surroundings of pickles, cheese, pastry, sponge-cake, and fruit—all of which are gobbled with such avidity and speed as would do the highest credit to a flock of hungry geese. "All aboard!" cries the conductor. Then wooden toothpicks are snatched from the counter, seventy-five cents hastily paid to a gentleman who receives the cash at the door, and the passengers are again seated and speeding on in the train.

Soon many of us, wrapped in our muffling, and lolling in all sorts of postures, are attempting to doze ; but sleep we cannot ; for passengers are continually dropping out and coming in, and that tormenting official, the conductor, is ever and anon going his rounds, like a ghost, and poking us up, to examine or to clip a bit from our ticket. But as there is no use in grumbling, we try to make the best of affairs ; and so, between occasional napping, and thinking, and dreaming, and changing our posture, the monotonous hours of night wear away.

Morning is breaking, the grey shadows disappear before the paler light, and these again give place to the broad, bright, genial beams of the risen sun and, as we speed along, eyes are rubbed, limb stretched, dress somewhat adjusted, and sundry inquiries addressed to the conductor as to when and where we are to stop for the morning meal. Our European eyes are strained to catch a sight of the rare beauty, the grandeur, the overwhelming sublimity, as we have been led to expect, of the American landscape.

But we are much disappointed. The bright azure above is transparently clear, and upon either hand are broad-stretching fields in faded verdure ; for it is early autumn, and the freshness of the fair young spring, like the charms of many other beauties, has long since passed away. Trees are not so numerous as we expected, nor so beautiful, while many of the

meadows and sloping hills are disfigured by grim pro-
truding stumps. The farmsteads, built of wood, are
neat, with verandahs and trellises, and green Venetian
blinds. Generally they are painted buff or beautifully
white, but some of them are dingy brown. A few are
mere shanties, and miserably poor. The villages—
with church and schoolhouse attached—straggle;
each building standing on a "lot" by itself. Then,
with wooden houses, there are wooden palings, wooden
fences, wooden side-walks ; in fact, almost wooden
everything, so that this wooden sameness tires and
palls upon the eye.

By the way, we have been much amused by reading
the following, from the pen of one of our transatlantic cousins, on "English as compared with
American Scenery." The writer says :—"I may here
say that one great disadvantage for any person desiring
to look at an English landscape is the absence of
good fences to sit upon ; the ground is usually too
damp to permit one to lie at full length. I missed
very much the rail fences of my own country. I
would come to a pretty prospect, and, my legs sinking
under me, I would look about for a place to sit. The
inhospitable landscape had not a single suggestion.
There were no stones, and a hedge was of course not
to be thought of. How different the stake-and-rider
fences of this land of ours ! The top rail of a good
fence is as fine a seat as one can wish. Of course,
much depends upon the shape and position of the
rail. Sometimes the upper rail is sharp and knotted.
But one has only to walk on for a rod or two, before

a perfect seat can be found, and this point I have
discovered to be the very best from which the scene
may be viewed. It really seems as if the honest
farmer had builded better than he knew. If there is
one place from which to overlook a landscape to be
preferred to another, I have always found that Nature,
so far from betraying him that loved her, had actually
put there the properly shaped rail at his disposal."—

"I missed very much the rail fences of my own .
country . . . the stake-and-rider fences of this land
of ours."—Indeed, my friend, did you? Then, if so,
you missed a great deal of ugliness; for nothing so
mars the rustic beauty, the landscape naturalness and
harmony of this land of yours as these same brownish-
white, staring, stalking, straggling stake-and-rider
fences which bestride the land, and which have
nothing whatever to justify their existence save the
plea of unavoidable need.

To us American scenery, as compared with English,
seems as the large, bold, beautiful cartoon, compared
with the smaller, but complete and exquisitely finished
picture. For, amid the broad plains and swelling
hills, we miss the massive stone rural mansion, with
its well-laid-out gardens, its trim green lawn, its
shrubs and noble trees; the compact hamlet, with its
white gables and ancient Gothic spire, nestling in
umbrageous leaves; the green hedge-row and mossy .
ditch, with enamelling of wild flowers and warbling
music of the feathered tribes; the neat, though
humble, cottage, fronted by the variegated and
fragrant floral knot, and garlanded in woodbine

twined with many a white and scarlet rose; and the mediæval castle, grey with age, yet clad in the frondal beauty of joyful ivy, and rich in legendary lore.

Time will, no doubt, confer upon America many of these elements of landscape enchantment; but there are others of them which the rigour of her climate must for ever deny. Yet she has beauties peculiar to herself, and with which her people may be well content; for, in the grandeur of her far-extending plains, the sublime elevation of her mountains,—in the magnificence of her lakes, forests, and rivers,—in her rushing cataracts, and the gorgeous colouring of her autumnal leaves;—where shall we go to find her equal?

Morning and noon glide pleasantly away. But in the afternoon, forgetting that our train starts without previous note of bell or whistle, and not having heard the usual "All aboard!" we are nearly left behind at a restaurant in which we have dined. The train is moving as we reach the platform, and the breaksman, a round-faced, sly-looking darky, shows his sympathy by laughing aloud at our mishap. But roused by the thought of being left 400 miles short of our journey, we rush forward, seize the rail, jump on the square platform behind, and so escape the awkward predicament of being left in the lurch. Yet Mr. Darky never puts out his brawny hand to help us, but looks as if he thought a good joke was spoiled by our being able to get in. For darkies are too often sly, witty, and over fond of practical fun. We remember on one occasion, when dining in a hotel at Philadelphia, an ebony waiter spilled a lot of white pudding-sauce

down the back of our coat, of which he said nothing;
though, we suspect, he must have amused himself
during the evening, as he saw us moving about among
a large company of strangers to whom the stripes
along the back of our costume must have looked
ludicrously queer.

Having passed through New York State, part of
Pennsylvania, part of Ohio, and part of Indiana, we,
on the second morning of our journey, enter South
Bend; nor are we very much fatigued after so lengthy
a run. A shabby omnibus brings us, through dense
clouds of suffocating dust and over an unmacadamised
road, to our hotel; where we are regaled with a good
wash and a simple morning meal.

The town is a smart one, with a goodly number of
stores, churches, and, I am sorry to add, drinking
saloons. But the country around is miserably flat.
The fields are covered over with tall coarse stalks of
Indian corn, and diversified here and there with great
orange-looking pumpkins, and with patches of whitish
verdure. There are a good many houses of the usual
American style—frame, with verandahs, ornamental
trellises, and Venetian blinds; and not a few of them
have an air not only of comfort, but of luxury and
wealth. But how poor the patches of garden
around them. Here are flower-beds without flowers,
bordered with narrow unsightly boards—filled with
coarse arid stalks and long rank grass—and surrounded with languid-looking shrubs and trees. But
how could a delicate vegetation flourish in this place?
On the day of our arrival so broiling is the heat that

every move brings a gush of perspiration from our pores; next day the air is chilled by a white, biting frost; the following day is cold, with torrents of rain; and the day after is so impregnated with an icy dampness that it obliges us not only to don our over-coat, but to button it as high up to the chin as we can. Such atmospheric vicissitudes are not friendly to flowers and delicate plants; though they are—as the Southbenders most certainly told us—to fever, chills, ague, and a most distressing form of catarrh.

But the place is more stirring than it usually is; for the Conference of the Methodist Episcopal Church is in session here, and its ministers, many of whom have come afar, are enjoying the proffered hospitality of the rising town. For us the proceedings of the Conference have very much interest, for we have not as yet seen such an assembly on American soil. Let us go and have a glimpse.

The place of session is a commodious and well-furnished school-room in the basement of a very fine church, built of red brick, and ornamented with a lofty and handsome spire. There might be about 130 ministers present, who occupy the front seats; those behind affording accommodation to the public, who attend in considerable numbers, and who, in America, are never excluded when any of the numerous Methodist Conferences in that country have met. The bishop presides, while two or three secretaries sit behind desks near his chair.

Devotional exercises ended, and the roll called over, almost all the members of the Conference seem nomi-

nated on various committees, to whom a very large
part of the business is entrusted, and who, in due
time, are to present their reports. On a great variety
of matters, each presiding elder reports for the district
under his care ; and as the reports of committees
come up, or as miscellaneous resolutions are offered,
they are fully, freely, and fairly discussed. Indeed,
in this, and in several other Conferences which we had
the privilege of subsequently attending, we were
much struck with the freedom and fairness of discussion that in every instance took place. Of course,
exciting and sharply-debated questions turned up,
from time to time, and, sometimes, questions in which
the presiding officers themselves felt the deepest
interest ; yet we never observed an American bishop
exhibit the slightest excitement or impatience, or
interject his opinion in the midst of a debate. Nor
have we known a bishop to deliver his own judgment
on any matter in debate until after the vote of the
Conference was had. Such things, it is true, may
sometimes have happened ; but during our attendance
at several Conferences in various parts of the country,
we do not remember to have witnessed any such case.
Indeed, what we have seen of the American bishops
in the Conferences has produced the impression on
our minds that they are able administrators, impartial
moderators of assemblies, thorough gentlemen in their
bearing and language, and approachable as children
by both ministers and people.

    During this session an animated and almost im-
passioned discussion takes place on a resolution

virtually condemnatory of the appointments of several
of the presiding elders, which must have been exciting
to the bishop, inasmuch as the sole right of making
such appointments is invested in himself. Yet he
manifests no feeling, expresses no opinion, and ex-
hibits no uneasiness about the apparent infringement
of his constitutional rights ; though the resolution is
carried, and obliges the removal of several presiding
elders from their office.

This discussion, and a good deal that we subsequently heard, impressed us with the fact that, on
the whole, the presiding elders are an unpopular
class in the Methodist Episcopal Church. Several of
these whom we met seemed excellent and estimable
men. Yet many persons in America, especially those
belonging to the older and best organized churches,
evidently look upon the whole class as so many drones
in the hive, or as so much ecclesiastical lumber of
which they would very willingly get rid.

Three public services, besides many others in
various parts of the town, are conducted in the Conference Church ; each of which is attended by a large,
intelligent, and devout-looking concourse of people.
As many as 1,500 might be present, all of whom, led
by a small organ, engage in singing the praises of
God. And such singing—so general, so true to time,
and so sweetly harmonious—we have seldom heard.

Illness prevents the bishop from preaching. His
place, however, is well filled by an able doctor, at
the forenoon service. We thought the afternoon
sermon, preached by another doctor, poor and pe-

dantic ; and the discourse in the evening, though intensely earnest, seemed exceedingly vapid, tedious, and in some of its utterances singularly queer. What would Old-Country folks think of such appeals as this ?—"Brothers and sisters, I appeal to you ! Men and women, I appeal to you ! Ladies and gentlemen, I appeal to you !"—and all this, with a good deal more of the same kind, uttered in loud, half-scream-ing tones, and accompanied by uncouth and gro-tesquely extravagant gesticulation.

But when we thought of the labours of these men, the work they had accomplished, the noble living churches which, by God's help, they had created, and the commodious, elegant, and, in some cases, imposing structures they had erected, we could not but feel that, notwithstanding some individual oddi-ties, they commanded our respect, veneration, and love.

The Conference closes its sittings, at the end of a week, with the reading of the appointments by the bishop, whose judicious, wise, and fraternal counsels we cannot easily forget. But how is it that all American Conferences, however large, and however weighted with business, manage to get through, with-out even the appearance of hurry, and with the fullest liberty of discussion, in the course of a week ? Of course we do not speak of the General Conference, whose proceedings we have not had an opportunity to note.

CHAPTER VI.

FROM South Bend we return to New York. Meantime, we turn aside, and have a peep at the Falls. The town of Niagara is reached at midnight. Here we are ushered into a large square room of a commodious hotel. In the middle of the floor is the usual big American stove radiating a genial glow, of which we gladly avail ourselves, as the night is cold.

A round little man is sitting in front, whose short small-clothes, long grey stockings, and musical brogue give sure indication of whence he has come. "You,"— we venture to remark,—"are from the Old Country." Never shall we forget the suspicious, searching, half-frightened look of our new acquaintance, upon hearing these words. A momentary pause ensues, after which he replies :—"How do *you* know?" Soon after the round little fellow shuffles from his seat by the stove, and makes quietly off; leaving the uncharitable impression on our minds, that he is one of those patriotic souls who leave their country for their country's good, and that he has a rational fear of being ungraciously pounced upon by some disguised and disagreeably inquisitive detective.

Up in the morning, and away to the Falls. But it

is an ugly morning of scowling clouds and mizzling rain ; and by no means favourable for seeing the mammoth cataract, the thunder of whose waters is already sounding in our ears. Time, however, is precious, and the opportunity must not be lost ; moreover, the rain is clearing off and the horizon brightening; and so, with a couple of companions, we jump into a carriage engaged for the occasion, and start.

Our first glimpse of the rushing and thundering waters is somewhat disappointing ; for the Falls are not so high, so wide, so deep, so astounding as imagination and description had led us to expect. And so, with some abatement of our quickened pulsations, we roll on to the toll-bridge, cross it, and find ourselves gliding amid the witching sylvan scenes of Goat Island ; which, as everybody knows, stands at the head of the twofold cataract, dividing the broad waters of the mighty Niagara river in twain.

But after all that has been said of Niagara, who shall attempt to describe it again ? Certainly not ourselves ; for we feel humbly conscious that neither our prose or poetry is equal to the task. Yet we may be permitted to say that, as we gaze upon the aqueous masses gliding, rushing, eddying, gurgling, foaming, plunging, and, again, rebounding in cloudy vapours from the depths beneath ; and, as we listen to the deep full volume of their everlasting roar ; we feel as if transported to another world, whose scenes and surroundings are at once so strange, so dreamily weird, so beautiful, so grand, as to excite within us mysterious and rapturous emotions of mingling wonder, admiration, delight, and awe.

But one of our companions will have us go down the American Fall. We demur. "But," it is urged, "here is an opportunity in a lifetime. It will not occur again. So you had better come." Well then, here goes ; for it will be something to get under the falling torrents, and something to say that we were there.

So we enter a small house perched on the side of the rocky precipice that overlooks the Falls ; and then, under due instructions from the man in charge, we undergo a thorough metamorphosis. Each, like one conducted to a prison, is put into a cell-like apartment by himself. We are asked about our money, jewelry, and such like things, and ordered to deposit them in something like a strong tin cash-box ; which, when done, the box is locked, and its key is suspended by a piece of twine round our neck. Then comes off all the covering with which art has supplemented nature ; and a woollen suit—stockings, drawers, vest, all well aired, but none well fitting—is put on. A casing of yellow oil-cloth follows, like the knightly armour of the olden time ; only our feet, instead of being encased in mail, are clad in felt, tightly tied with hempen cords. Our guide, a fine athletic Canadian, is clad in similar attire.

And now we start. Following our mentor, we reach a precipitous gallery or stairs, formed of rough plank, and covering the side of a swift-descending cliff. Reaching the foot of this, we get to a rock,

F

along which we proceed horizontally, until we reach
the open top of a square tower made of wood. Into
this we venture, and, having reached its bottom by a
winding staircase, we again emerge in open air. Our
way is now along a narrow, almost goat-like path,
where we begin to feel 'the wetting spray, and to
realise the advantage of our felt shoes, which prevent
us from slipping and swiftly shooting from the rock
to the deep abyss beneath. Pausing here, we are
impressed with the grandeur of the great Canadian
Fall, which now is pretty full in view. Gazing
upward, we see ourselves overhung and overshadowed
by mighty wall-like cliffs that rear their tops towards
the sky ; and, looking downward, we behold these
same rocks bathing their rugged fronts in boiling and
eddying floods of snowy foam. Our path, now sloping
gently downward, becomes narrower and narrower, so
that, at length, our quivering nerves compel us to
inform our guide that we can proceed no farther
without serious risk.   Soon, however, we are assured
by the firm grasp of the bold Canadian, who clasps
his hand in ours, and we continue to descend.

But where is our adventurous friend ? Behind and
above us we see him screwing his way downwards,
with hands and haunches alternately resting upon
and ignominiously rubbing the crumbling rock. Descending further, we reach a narrow wooden door,
through which we pass, and from which, amid blinding
showers of spray, we walk along some rough-cut
planks, guarded by a rail, which we gladly hold.

At length we reach the lowest depths ; and passing

in between the face of the bare wet rock and the
swift-descending flood, we calmly take our stand.
How strange the scene! The rocky wall behind ;—
the mighty cataract above ;—the din, the roar, the
splashing fall all round ;—the descending deluge ;—
the foaming floods. Have we reached another planet?
Or do we dream?

Our ascent is, of course, by the same route as that
by which we reached the bottom of the Fall. When
about half way up, two figures, strange and startling
to look upon, approach us in the distance. Who, we
ask ourselves, are these? Can they be Indians of
whom we have heard so much, but whom as yet we
have not seen? For a moment we stare, and almost
shrink. Pooh! these are a pair of fools, who, like
ourselves, have paid their dollars for the chance of
tumbling headlong from the rocks, and finding a final
resting-place in the depths below. But their appearance makes us realise, for the first time, how strange
a figure we ourselves must make, since our attire is
exactly similar to theirs.

And now, well heated by our climbing, we reach
the place from which we first set out. We therefore
doff our borrowed suit, and having quietly made our
toilet in the little cell-like room, we start along a
path of wild and witching beauty in the direction of
the river above the great Canadian Fall. Here, amid
encircling rush and foam, we step on to the rocky
islets called "The Sisters;" where, in view of
Nature's most imposing and fascinating grandeur,
we sit down to muse. Behind us is the mighty river,

—broad and deep, fringed with rich and many-tinted frondal splendour, marking the territorial limits of two free and mighty nations, and ever hurrying onward to the boundless sea. Wide and lofty is the dome above us, though just now somewhat dull with greyish mist. Before us the waters,—swift and glassy, save where they foam against some obstructive rocky mass,—are rushing to their deep, dark leap ; while from the abyss beyond, uprising clouds of spray that mingle with the ethereal mists above and never-ceasing thunder tell of the headlong torrents that have plunged below. Now we think of far-off home and those we love, wishing they, too, were here to share the pleasure of the wondrous scene ; and now, we think of Old England's giant poet, who so grandly sang :—

> " These are Thy glorious works, Parent of good,
>   Almighty ! Thine this universal frame,
>   Thus wondrous fair : Thyself how wondrous then,
>   Unspeakable ! who sittest above these heavens
>   To us invisible, or dimly seen
>   In these Thy lowest works."

And as the sublime is seldom, with us mortals, far from the ridiculous, we are reminded of a story told us in New York. Once, says our informant, a coloured preacher illustrated the danger of a sinner by the condition of one borne onward by the swift waters of Niagara, and fast approaching the terrific Fall. "Dar he is ! Dar he is ! "—shouted the impassioned preacher. " Bredren, blow up de Gospel trumpet : blow up de Gospel trumpet : blow it up. Blow up de

Gospel trumpet; for de sinner is getting near de Fall. See, bredren, he is going over. Over! Over! —He is gone!—*Grabitation* and *suctation tucked* him down!" Though we smile at the peculiar phraseology of our coloured friend, yet the illustration is apt enough. For, alas! too many, hurried on-ward by their passions, or by their sordid interests, or by both, are ever rushing to a more appalling doom than he is, who, borne on the tide before us, goes with its swift dark waters to the depths beyond. But time flies, and we may not linger. So, with regretful feelings, we break off our solitary com-munings, and turn away from these enchanting scenes.

Soon again—in the usual cars, with the usual ever-changing fellow-travellers, and amid the usual inci-dents—we are speeding eastward to the great city of New York. But O, how mortifying! In changing our cars, we have taken the wrong train ; and, as the consequence of our error, we are compelled to spend nearly a whole day at Elmira. This is a good town ; where,—between loitering at the depot, slowly pacing the streets, gazing at the churches, which are nume-rous and good-looking, and at the private houses, many of which are indicative of wealth and taste, and reading the newspapers,—we get through the tardy hours as best we can.

In the evening we are on the platform in good time, awaiting the arrival of the train. But what crowds are gathering ;—crowds, too, that very much remind us by their appearance and manner of the well-to-do farming classes of the north of Ireland, when decked out in holiday attire. Indeed, but for the high-pitched, semi-nasal tone, and the absence of Scotch idiomatic phrase, vocalization, and accent, we might almost fancy ourselves at a Belfast railway terminus, at the close of some large fair or agricultural show.

But what do these crowds mean ? The spacious waiting-rooms are full, the platform full ; and still they come thronging through every avenue of ingress that can anywhere be found,—talking, and laughing, and jostling, but, to their credit be it said, none brawling, and hardly any obviously under the influence of intoxicating drink.

Curiosity prompts us to inquire,—" Why this crowd ?" We learn that Barnum has been in town, and that all the country has gathered to do admiring homage to his show. Suddenly we ask ourselves, what if a quarrel should now arise ? What if the pleasure-seeking excitement of the day should find its climax in a row ? How could it be quelled ? How could order be restored ? In what or in whom could the weak find protection from the violence or rapacity of the strong ? For here are no police, no military, no formidable array of stalwart railway officials—in fact, no one with the slightest appearance of authority, much less of authority backed by organized force. For some time we keep revolving this problem, and, at length, come to the conclusion that the American people are sober and orderly ; and though the country is too often startled by deeds of violence, robbery, and blood, yet such deeds would be even more frequent in the Old Country, if its police were as scanty and as ill-organized as that of the United States. Nor do we think the English gipsy is much astray in his opinions, when—according to the representation of his lyrical friends and admirers—he embodies them in such elegant poetical effusions as this :—

> " The 'Merican land, I think, mayhap,
> Is just the spot for a Rommany chap ;
> For, from all I hears, there they lives at peace,
> An' the people don't care for no police."

At length the train has arrived. A rush, and the cars are filled ; and once more our iron horses, puffing and rattling, are pulling us along towards the heralding shadows of night in the East.

CHAPTER VII.

THE Empire City is more than usually moved. Good men, wise men, religious men—pastors of churches, professors of colleges, missionary secretaries —the best men, lay and cleric, of the manifold Protestant denominations—all are consulting, planning, arranging with zealous animation and thoughtful care. For the Evangelical Alliance is about to hold its "Sixth General Conference," and places of meeting are to be prepared for its sessions. Moreover, the Christians from afar—many of them men of mark in the churches, the universities, and the nations to which they belong—are to be tendered the rites of hospitality ; and the generous citizens of the Great Republic—her churches, her civic authorities, her railroad companies, and even her great officers of state are resolved that that hospitality shall be on a scale of cordiality and munificence worthy of the name and resources of the American people. And so, indeed, it subsequently turns out to be ; for who that witnessed it can ever forget the courtesy, the kindness, the fraternal regard, and the exuberant affluence of hospitality shown to the foreign delegates and other visitors on that great and memorable occasion ?

And now that the evening of the 2nd October, the time of meeting, has come, we find our way to a "Social Reunion of Members and Invited Guests." The place is Association Hall, a noble building erected by the Young Men's Christian Association of the City of New York; and containing, besides a spacious audience-room, ample and well-furnished reception-rooms, a large library, and many other convenient and valuable apartments.

The walls are adorned with numerous and skilfully executed paintings; and amongst others, we are glad to observe a full-length portrait of Her Most Gracious Majesty Queen Victoria, in a magnificent gilt frame, and hung in a position where every one who enters may see it. After all, we think the Americans are not such national bigots, and such dreadful haters of perfidious Albion, as the sayings of speculating political knaves and blustering demagogues sometimes represent them to be; for who can reconcile this bigotry and hatred with the honour thus done to our Queen?

The well-lit and handsome apartments are soon crowded with such a cosmopolitan gathering of well-dressed, well-mannered, well-pleased Christian people as, perhaps, the world has seldom, if ever, seen—the ladies, as always happens on such occasions, being largely and well represented; while—intermingled with smiles, bowings, hand-shakings, and friendly salutations—a babble of conversation, in English, French, Italian, German, Dutch, and other languages, makes the whole area resound, like a swarming hive amid the glowing radiance of a summer day.

An hour after, and we are in the audience-room—a fine apartment with spacious galleries and platform, and the ground-floor of which is accommodated with long rows of comfortable seats. From a volume since published by the Alliance in America the following extract will, no doubt, be interesting to our readers :—

"Soon every seat was filled, and every inch of available standing-room was occupied. Half of the ground-floor was reserved for the use of the delegates, and on the platform were seated the president and many of the other officers of the United States Alliance, and such of the delegates as were to take part in the services of the evening.

"It is not often that one is permitted to gaze upon such a sight as was then presented. The hall itself was tastefully decorated. The platform was carpeted, and adorned with evergreens, flowers, and plants. In the centre of the wall behind the platform were the initials and motto of the Alliance, with the date of its organization, and the date of the present Conference :

𝔈. 𝔄.

UNUM CORPUS SUMUS IN CHRISTO.

1846.   1873.

"Just below this was the motto, also descriptive of the principles of the Alliance, 'In Necessariis Unitas ; in Dubiis Libertas ; in Omnibus Caritas.'

Around these mottoes the names of the eminent reformers and theologians, Luther, Calvin, Wycliffe, Edwards, Knox, Bunyan, and Wesley, were arranged. On the balcony was the Greek name of the fish 'ΙΧΘΥΣ, the mystic emblem of the faith of the early Christians in the days of their persecution, containing, as it does, the initial letters of the words in which they confessed Jesus Christ, the Son of God, as their Saviour, 'Ιησοῦς 'Χριστὸς Θεοῦ 'Υιὸς Σωτήρ.

"From the ceiling above the platform the flag of the Union was gracefully festooned, to which was appended the shield containing our national motto, "E Pluribus Unum"—a motto equally appropriate to the united Christian body under whose auspices the festivities of the evening were celebrated. On either side of the American flag, completing the drapery, were the flags of Great Britain, France, and Germany.

"At the other end of the hall, on the front of the gallery, were the first and last letters of the Greek alphabet, applied by Christ to Himself in the last chapter of Revelation, ΑΩ."

The Hon. William E. Dodge, President of the United States Alliance, is moved by acclamation to the chair. Then follows the singing of the hymn commencing :—

> " From all who dwell below the skies,
> Let the Creator's praise arise ;
> Let the Redeemer's name be sung
> Through every land, by every tongue."

And how grand it is when these sublime words are

sung by the united voices of representatives from
almost all nations from India to Britain, and from
Britain to the shores of the Pacific Ocean. As the
organ peals forth, in rich and powerful tones, its ac-
companiment, in the music of the "Old Hundredth,"
aiding, and softly blending with, the vocal harmony
of the entire audience,

> "Let the Redeemer's name be sung
> Through every land, by every tongue,"——

the words seem no longer the expression of a pious
wish or of a devout prophetic yearning, but a realised
sublimity, upon which myriads of unseen spirits look
with enraptured gaze; and, as they look, are stimulated
to attune their harps and voices to a strain more
exalted and thrilling than that in which it is their
wont to sing.

The full and sweetly-modulated music ended, the
Rev. C. Dallas Marston, M.A., of London, leads the
devout and responsive assembly in the Lord's Prayer.

Then follows an address of welcome from the Rev.
William Adams, D.D., LL.D., of New York, which
for ripe intelligence, warm cordiality, and touching
pathos is all that could be wished ; and which elicits
pleasing, and in some instances eloquent, responses
from Lord Alfred Churchill and Dr. Stoughton, of
London ; the Rev. Dr. Fisch, of Paris ; the Rev. Dr.
Coulin, of Geneva ; Professor Dornor, of the University of Berlin ; Professor Theodore Christlieb, of the
University of Bonn ; the Rev. Narāyan Sheshādri, of
India ; and a good many more.

During the address of the Prussian Christlieb, a rather dramatic effect is produced by his advancing towards the French Fisch, with outstretched hand, and saying—"There are times—and this is one of them—when Germans can, in a sense, forget that they are Germans, and shake hands with their French brethren. The fathers of our faith are already one before the throne, and their children should be one." Fisch, rising from his seat, accepts the proffered hand. Yet, to us, his somewhat downcast eye and half-averted look seem to say—"What grace it needs to enable one to look lovingly into the eyes of a man belonging to a people by whose vengeful power one's nation has been smitten and struck down." Nārāyan Sheshādri is a converted Brahmin of sable hue, whose flowing oriental robe and snowy turban contrast picturesquely with the European and American costumes around him. We believe he is a convert and a missionary of the Presbyterian Church. Certainly, he is a Christian of rare intelligence and piety, with a surprising facility of apt and impressive speech. Indeed, for a foreigner, he seems to have acquired a wondrous mastery of our Anglican tongue.

The benediction, pronounced by a New York minister, brings the delightful exercises of the evening to a close, and the immense assemblage begins to file slowly along towards the wide-open doors that lead to the street. Suddenly, the organ peals forth, as we suppose, "God save the Queen." But, no ; we are mistaken. The music is, indeed, that of our National Anthem ; but it has been appropriated by our trans-

atlantic cousins, who style it "America," and who
pay us the compliment of adapting it to the following,
which may be regarded as their national anthem, if,
indeed, they have any such anthem at all.

> " My country, 'tis of thee,
>   Sweet land of liberty,
>   Of thee I sing :
>   Land where my fathers died ;
>   Land of the pilgrim's pride ;
>   From every mountain side
>   Let freedom ring.
>
> " My native county ! thee;
>   Land of the noble free,
>   Thy name I love :
>   I love thy rocks and rills,
>   Thy woods and templed hills ;
>   My heart with rapture thrills
>   Like that above.
>
> " Let music swell the breeze,
>   And ring from all the trees
>   Sweet freedom's song !
>   Let mortal tongues awake ;
>   Let all that breath partake ;
>   Let rocks their silence break—
>   The sound prolong !
>
> " Our Father's God ! to Thee,
>   Author of liberty,
>   To Thee we sing ;
>   Long may our land be bright
>   With freedom's holy light;
>   Protect us by Thy might,
>   Great God, our King ! "

Next morning we find our way to Steinway Hall, a
great music-hall, in which the formal organization of

the Conference is to take place. The appointed hour is ten o'clock ; but long before this the building is packed, as some would say, from the floor to the ceiling—the ground-floor, balconies, and platform, presenting one dense array of human heads. Human heads, too, representing the intelligence, the piety, and the Christian amity of almost all nations ; for, though the great mass are Americans, there are present, besides the accredited foreign delegates, Christian missionaries from Burmah, Siam, China, Ceylon, India, Turkey, Syria, Egypt, and South Africa.

And from all these what a volume of praise ascends to the Triune Jehovah, as by the lips of the Hon. William E. Dodge the last words are uttered of—

> " Praise God, from whom all blessings flow,
> Praise Him, all creatures here below ;
> Praise Him above, ye heavenly host,
> Praise Father, Son, and Holy Ghost."

An eminent and venerable Presbyterian professor, the Rev. Dr. Hodge, of Princeton, leads in prayer ; a portion of Scripture, the seventeenth chapter of the Gospel by St. John, is read by an English Methodist minister, the Rev. James H. Rigg, D.D., of London ; and the Very Rev. Dr. Smith, Dean of Canterbury, repeats the Apostles' Creed.

And surely the recital of this noble *Credo* is a thing to be remembered for ever. The whole audience are standing ; and as, slowly, solemnly, and

distinctly, the venerable dean utters the grand old
Catholic formula, each word is caught up and
repeated by the living, intelligent, and immortal
masses, until the very building itself seems instinct
with living Christian truth, and yearning with the
hope of " the life everlasting." Talk of sublimity!
What have we seen so sublime as this? We have
seen the wide expanse of ever-rolling sea, roofed by the
azure sky, and rimmed by the far and dim horizon; we
have seen great Niagara with its rush, its everlasting thunder, and its falling floods; we have seen the
Rocky Mountains swelling from the plains in awful
grandeur, and burying their snowy heads within the
clouds above; we have seen in the deep shadows of
the night the boundless prairie glowing and flaming
far and near with encircling fire; we have seen—sub-
limest of all sublimities in nature!—above the plains
of Nebraska, the starry host—"worlds on worlds!
amazing pomp!"—hung in lustrous glory from the
cloudless void. Yes, all these we have seen; and we
have pronounced them sublime. Yet their aggregate
sublimity seems to us less impressive, less imposing,
less intensely moving than this great world-repre-
sentative assembly of all Evangelical churches, uniting
with one heart and one voice in this ancient and
comprehensive summary of " the faith which was
once delivered unto the saints."

Prayer follows, in which the vast assembly is led
by an Italian minister; and then again, accompanied
by the pealing tones of a powerful organ, the whole
audience thunder forth—

" All hail the power of Jesus' name !
Let angels prostrate fall.
Bring forth the royal diadem,
And crown Him Lord of all.

" Let high-born seraphs tune the lyre,
And as they tune it, fall
Before His face, who formed their choir,
And crown Him Lord of all.

" Ye souls redeemed of Adam's race,
Ye ransom'd from the fall;
Hail Him who saves you by His grace,
And crown Him Lord of all.

" O, that with yonder sacred throng,
We at His feet may fall;
There join the everlasting song,
And crown Him Lord of all ! "

Speeches follow, in one of which is set forth the astounding fact that " The population of this city in which we are convened has, within the life of men present here to-day, grown from 70,000 to about 1,000,000, while the population of the United States has in the same time increased from 6,000,000 to 40,000,000."

The list of delegates having been read, the Conference elects as its president, Dr. Theodore Woolsey, of New Haven, Connecticut. An address from Dr. Woolsey follows, in which, among other things, he states, "A German antiquary says that, in Cæsar's time, a squirrel could jump from tree to tree, from the Rhine to the Elbe. So, two hundred and fifty years ago, an almost unbroken forest stretched from the Atlantic to the Pacific, roamed over by a few

G

Pagans. Now, in these United States, more than
60,000 Protestant churches attest to the diffusive
energy of the Gospel."

After the President's address, rules are adopted for
the regulation of the future proceedings of the
Conference, and reports on the state of religion in
Italy and Germany are listened to with the attention
and interest which their importance demands.

But it is one o'clock, the sitting must close ; and
so Steinway Hall is willingly abandoned for Association Hall, where an enormous mass of delicious
swallowing material is heaped on well-arranged and
well-served tables in the lecture-room and library, for
the purpose of repairing frail tenements somewhat
impaired by the wear and tear of a rather sultry day.
We say, an enormous mass. And we say truly ; for,
right, left, centre, all round, are piles of ham sandwiches, piles of beef sandwiches, piles of bread and
butter, piles of cake—hard cake, soft cake, jam cake,
butter cake, sweet cake ; and for washing all this
down, there is an immense provision of tea, coffee,
and delicious ice-cream. And all this is renewed day
by day during the sittings of the Conference, and to
the delegates it is free of charge. Surely, such
thoughtful and abounding hospitality does high credit
to the head, hands, and heart of Christian America.

During nine subsequent days (the Sundays excepted) sittings are simultaneously held in three or
four places, when papers are read and conversations
take place on the state of religion in various coun-
tries, Christian union, Christianity and its anta-

gonisms, personal and family religion, education and literature, the pulpit of the age, and a great many other kindred topics. These sessions, together with other meetings of a more strictly devotional nature, create a deep interest in the public mind, and are attended by constantly increasing crowds, so that towards the close of the Conference ingenuity fails to find accommodation for all who seek admission to the halls and churches in which the proceedings are carried on.

On two occasions the foreign delegates, in a long array of carriages, are driven out for an airing— once to Greenwood Cemetery and once to Central Park ; they are hospitably entertained at a public dinner in the Academy of Music in Brooklyn, which is followed by a most enthusiastic public meeting ; and they are most generously presented with tickets by the Erie, Pennsylvania, and other railway companies, for the purpose of travelling free of cost on their lines. Moreover, they are taken on an excursion by the Mayor and Corporation of New York, with whom they subsequently dine on Ward's Island. Surely, on this memorable occasion, America did herself immortal honour, and set an example of warmhearted and munificent generosity, which it is to be hoped the nations of Europe will not be slow to follow.

But as all things human have an end, so, on Sunday night, ten days after the Conference opened, its last meeting is held in the Academy of Music. Here, in the presence of an immense multitude of highly interested and deeply moved Christian people, many touching utterances of farewell are spoken, after which the following doxology is sung :—

> " To God the Father, God the Son,
> And God the Spirit, three in one,
> Be honour, praise, and glory given,
> By all on earth, and all in heaven."

Dr. Edmund S. Janes, senior bishop of the Methodist Episcopal Church, pronounces the benediction ; and the vast assembly separates, never to come together again until the blast of the archangel's trump shall summon the sleeping dead from their graves, and all the elect of God are gathered together in one to be visibly united to and glorified with Jesus their divine Saviour and Head for ever.

CHAPTER VIII.

THE stream of American hospitality continues to flow. The foreign delegates are invited to Philadelphia and Washington ; and to visit the President of the United States, who has kindly signified his willingness to receive them, and to give them a hearty welcome in the name of the American people. Moreover, Princeton University has invited them to call by the way, that they may have a peep at that place of learning, long since so honoured by the name of Jonathan Edwards, and now so honoured by the name and services of the illustrious Dr. M'Cosh.

It is our privilege to join the crowds of ladies and gentlemen that are rapidly filling the " palace cars " of a special train, generously provided free of cost by the Pennsylvania Railroad Company. And what a beautiful morning !—so calm, so clear, so sparkling with sun. And what a beautiful country, too ! Much of it is flat ; but it is luxuriantly fertile, and studded with substantial and picturesque villas. In the hazy distance are bluish hills, whose tranquil slopes and softly rounded tops gently undulate above the rim of the horizon ; while the foliage which everywhere meets the eye, varying in its colouring from the deep dark green of the solemn fir to the fiery glow of the autumnal maple, is gorgeous and enchanting.

Two hours bring us to Princeton, a beautiful rural-looking place, where we are met and kindly welcomed by the Faculties of the College and of the Theological Seminary ; and, as we pass from the train, a long file of manly-looking students line the road, and, with uncovered heads and waving hats, greet the strangers from afar with reiterated and ringing cheers.

Soon we are comfortably seated in the Second Presbyterian Church, where, during an hour, we are regaled with addresses from the Dean of Canterbury and others. Then, led by the venerable Dr. M'Cosh, we are conducted to the College, and, as we pass along, have pointed out to us the plain but comfortable home in which the celebrated Jonathan Edwards used to live. Nor do we fail to laugh outright as a venerable minister informs us of some shrewd celebrity, who, having read Edwards's famous work on the Human Will, laid down the book with mingled feelings of perplexity and anger, exclaiming : "There's a fallacy in it somewhere ; but it would take the devil himself to find it out."

Half an hour is spent in looking at and pacing through the buildings. Then an ample lunch, consisting of tea, coffee, sandwiches, confectionery, fruit, and never-failing ice-cream, is hastily swallowed ; after which, amid kindly and touching farewells, and the renewed and lusty cheering of young

America, we return to the railway cars, and speed onward to Philadelphia.

Upon our arrival in the city of Brotherly-love, we find a long array of two-horse open carriages waiting to convey us to Independence Hall, the building in which the fathers of American liberty had, nearly a hundred years before, signed the famous Declaration of Independence.

Narāyan Sheshādri, with dark face, and turbaned head, and loose flowing robe, sits prominently in the first carriage ; while the others, each furnished with four gazing and gazed-at occupants, file along slowly behind. Two of our companions, a pair of shrewd and humorous Germans, seem much amused at the curious stare of the people as we pass, and laughingly chat about the Barnum-like appearance of our charioted cavalcade.

But now that we are in the City Hall, words of kindly greeting are addressed to us by Judge Pierce, in behalf of the Mayor and Common Council of Philadelphia. As usual, speeches in reply follow. Then to "The Continental," a truly magnificent hotel, where, with munificent hospitality, the Philadelphia Branch of the Alliance treats us to an ample and luxurious dinner, though the tables are without wines or any other kind of alcoholic drink.

Dinner despatched with due expedition, let us stroll out and have a peep at the place. A fine city, truly, with broad, well-laid-out streets, numerous squares, and plenty of handsome churches, and other public buildings ; but, as might have been expected,

a long way behind New York. Many of the shops
are large and showy, and the private houses, though
generally built of brick, are, in some cases, faced
with marble. Everything has an air of remarkable
cleanliness and comfort. We are informed the population is about half a million ; many of whom find
employment in connection with the shipping of the
port, and in the manufacture of cotton, glass, and
other useful products of enterprising toil. · It is
obvious, too, that not a few of the fair denizens have
made goodly progress in the attainment of "Woman's
Rights ;" for we observe on the door-plates of several
of the houses—"Doctor Mary M——," "Doctor
Fanny B——," and such like.

The evening is spent at a large meeting in Horticultural Hall, a spacious building, highly decorated
for the occasion with flowers and evergreens, and
conspicuously mottoed with—"All one in Christ,"
"Let brotherly love continue," and many more of
a similar import. There are also adornments of
names in large and handsome letters, amongst which
are Huss, Wycliffe, Wesley, and Knox.

George H. Stuart, Esq., President of the Philadelphia Branch of the Alliance, and a nobly generous
Christian man, presides ; and, after devotional exercises, addresses the assembled crowds. Ex-Governor
Pollock, Bishop Simpson, and others, follow ; several
hymns being sung at intervals, in which the whole
assembly heartily join.

But O, the heat! How our pores give out.
Though it is the middle of October, seldom have we

been so stewed and simmered; no, not even when passing through the melting and panting purgatory of a Turkish bath. Yet there are no ladies screaming and fainting, and gently borne away on the stalwart arms of brothers, husbands, and other painfully anxious and deeply interested friends; which may perhaps be accounted for by the fact, that American ladies in general live like hot-house plants, being accustomed to the excessive heat of a burning sun in summer, and to the stoving of highly-heated houses in winter. Perhaps, too, their characteristic resolution and energy enable them to repel the squeamish and sentimental advances of fainting-fits in public.

Similar meetings are at the same time held in the Baptist and other churches; all of which are as crowded, as interesting, and as enthusiastic as the one in Horticultural Hall. How delightful to see such multitudes of Christian hearts belonging to all nations and evangelical denominations united in one common bond of Bible truth; and pouring forth a tide of fraternal Christian love in utterances of deep devotion at the common Mercy-Seat, in addresses of mutual sympathy and good will, and in harmonious and loud-resounding songs of loftiest praise to their one Divine and glorified Head.

Next morning we are on our way to Washington. A few hours bring us to Baltimore, where the delegates are met by a deputation, whose business is to take the strangers in charge as the guests of the Metropolitan Branch of the United States

Alliance. The mouthpiece of the deputation is Dr. S——, who wishes to deliver an address to the delegates. So every one is soon out on the platform, and the doctor, perched on the steps of one of the cars, is vociferously haranguing his audience, many of whom, amid the press and confusion, are unable to catch a single word he says. Suddenly the train moves slowly, carrying off the orator in the midst of his speech. "All aboard!" shouts the conductor. "All aboard!" echo a multitude of nervously excited voices; and the audience, startled by the thought of being left behind, rush and jostle in every direction; and, amid much disorder mingled with ejaculations of alarm and shouts of merriest laughter, all crush themselves into the cars as best they can. And so, once more, we are speeding along.

And now the metropolis of the great Republic is in view. Broad plains stretch out everywhere clad in autumnal verdure, and gaily plumed with tinted foliage of richest hues; the flowing waters of the broad and smooth Potomac are silvered with the radiance of a cloudless sun; the white dome of the Capitol, rising above dark tree-tops, stands boldly out from transparent depths of soft blue sky; and the sweet and far-sounding bells of the Metropolitan Methodist Episcopal Church are ringing out a joyous peal of welcome to the coming guests.

Soon we are at the depot, and are thence transferred by street-cars to Willard's, another of those splendid hotels of which America is full. Here the Rev. Dr. Tiffany and Governor Shepherd bid us welcome in kindest words.

But the President of the United States is waiting to receive us, and there must be no delay. And therefore, headed by the Governor and the District Secretary of Columbia, we proceed two-and-two in a line to the White House. What a plain, unpretending-looking residence it seems for so great a man! Lawn, trees, gardens, buildings —all remind us of the homely mansion of some country gentleman in our native land. As we approach we observe no guard, no sentinel, no lowly-bowing flunkey striped with gold and draped in plush. And now that we are in, everything seems substantial and snugly comfortable, without gilded grandeur or dazzling display.

And there stands the President himself—the chief magistrate of a mighty nation, the warrior who has drawn his sword in the sacred cause of liberty, the general whose skill and daring have brought him victory and fame. He looks a diffident and unassuming gentleman; with uncovered head, clad in plain black broadcloth, and unattended save by some of the members of the Cabinet, who take their stand by his side. At some distance behind are Mrs. Grant and some other ladies, whose curiosity, no doubt, prompts them to become spectators of the scene.

The Rev. Dr. Tiffany, of the Methodist Church, then delivers the following address :—

"Mr. President,—The Evangelical Alliance, which has been in session at New York, was a gathering of Christian men representing the Protestant faith. They came from many lands and uttered the mature thoughts of their churches ; they deliberated on topics of common interest to all Christians, and it is confidently believed that thus great stimulus has been given to Christian scholarship, enthusiasm awakened in Christian work, and the ties of Christian fellowship greatly strengthened. The churches and citizens have extended, through the local Metropolitan Branch of the Alliance, an invitation to the foreign delegation to visit the national capital. They have come in response to that invitation, accompanied by many American friends, and I now have the honour of presenting to the President of the United States and his Cabinet the officers and members of the Evangelical Alliance, but will first invite you to join in an invocation, led by the Dean of Canterbury, to our Heavenly Father."

Prayer is offered up by the Dean of Canterbury, at the conclusion of which the President, in his usual laconic style, replies as follows : "It affords me very great pleasure to welcome the Evangelical Alliance to the capital of this great nation, which I feel is the freest of nations, to work out the problem of your mission."

Then, advancing to where the President stands, we are severally introduced by name by George H. Stuart, Esq., of Philadelphia ; upon which the great

General shakes us cordially by the hand. This over, some short addresses follow, and we retire, very much pleased with the kindness of our reception, and with the common-sense simplicity of a Republican Court.

A peep at Washington follows. We find it much inferior not only to New York, but even to Philadelphia. But its streets, most of which run in straight lines, are of wondrous length and width, justifying the descriptive epithet so often applied to it,—"The city of magnificent spaces." Nor is the condition of these great thoroughfares up to the mark ; a fact which, we suppose, led an eminent minister from Edinburgh to say, in our hearing, to a large Washington audience, whose American virtues he was highly extolling : "Get your streets paved, and your roads mended, and you'll then be perfect." Nevertheless, it is a fine city, pleasantly situated, with some splendid public buildings, and containing a hundred thousand people.

In the evening we attend a crowded and enthusiastic meeting of the Alliance in the Metropolitan Methodist Episcopal Church, a handsome Gothic building, where the President and other members of the present Government usually worship. Similar meetings are at the same time held in the Presbyterian, Trinity Episcopal, and the Congregational Churches.

Next morning we visit the Capitol, which stands on a hill seventy feet above the Potomac river. It is a beautiful and stately Grecian structure, all of white marble, with lofty and imposing flights of steps, grand ornamental portico supported by Corinthian pillars, and broad and towering dome. It contains the House of Representatives, the Chambers of the Senate, the Congress Library, and the Supreme Court of the United States. Assembled within the area under the dome, and surrounded by its highly decorative mural paintings, the members of the Alliance and visitors strike up the hymn,— "All hail the power of Jesus' name!" The Lord's Prayer and the Apostles' Creed follow; after which is sung, " Praise God from whom all blessings flow."

At one o'clock we find ourselves at the hospitable banquet given by Governor Shepherd. Here, for the first time since coming to the States, we have wines on the table, most of which, however, are untouched by the guests. Surely, so far as strong drinks are concerned, the Americans are an abstemious people. True, they have drunkards among them—alas! too many. Yet, so far as we can observe, the people generally abhor the degrading and beastly vice of intoxication ; and are endeavouring, by total abstinence customs, example, and even rigid legislation, to banish drunkenness from their land. In this respect, they are—at least to a very great extent— worthy of our imitation.

The banquet over, and the speeches ended, some of the company go off to Richmond, for the purpose of visiting this memorable scene of the late intestine struggle. By the way, why is it that the people of the North are so unpatriotically silly as to keep open, by poetical recitals, speeches, and celebrations, the festering wounds inflicted by their late victory over the South ?

Yet so we have, with no little surprise, observed them to do. We very much fear the scenes and doings of such days as "Commemoration Day" must help to keep alive feelings which had better be buried; and so must the recital in schools of such pieces as that entitled "Sheridan's Ride," which closes with the following words :—

> "With foam and with dust the black charger was grey :
> By the flash of his eye, and his red nostrils' play,
> He seemed to the whole great army to say,
> I have brought you, Sheridan, all the way
> From Winchester down, to save the day.
> Hurrah, hurrah, for Sheridan !
> Hurrah, hurrah, for horse and man !
> And when their statues are placed on high,
> Under the dome of the Union sky,—
> The American soldier's temple of fame,—
> There, with the glorious general's name,
> Be it said in letters both gold and bright :
> ' Here is the steed that saved the day,
> By carrying Sheridan into the fight,
> From Winchester—twenty miles away.'"

No wonder people here feel deeply on the subject of the late Civil War ; but to what good end is such feeling to be continued ? It must eat like a canker into the body of the nation, and should be deprecated and avoided by every true Christian and every intelligent patriot. But this is a digression which we ask our readers to excuse.

Some others of the banqueted company wend their way westward, and not a few of us return to the

Empire City. We ourselves spend a night, on our way, in Baltimore, with an old and eloquent friend from the Emerald Isle, whose popularity here does not surprise us, for he has been popular everywhere; and whose large, costly, and exquisitely beautiful Gothic church we greatly admire. In this city there are more than 250,000 people, many of whom are Roman Catholics. The houses are built mostly of red brick; and to our eyes the place has an air of quietness and comfort, combined with many indications of intelligence and progress.

Next morning we are on our return journey to Philadelphia, and the following day we are again in New York.

CHAPTER IX.

TO THE PACIFIC.

IT is now getting late in November, and the weather
is just the reverse of what one could wish. Some days
are indeed fine; but these are few, and we have a
disagreeable variety of sleet, snow, rain, and skinning
visitations of razor-like winds. As might be sup-
posed from the nature of the weather, the streets are
anything but inviting; and as the flagging of the
footways, except in a few of the great thoroughfares,
is cracked, uneven, and pitted with little watery
hollows, the exercise of walking makes one unpleasantly acquainted with puddle, slush, and snow
intermingled with mud.

But why need we grumble? Since our stay is
nearly at an end, and we are soon to find our way to
California—that newly discovered paradise, of whose
perpetual sunshine, balmy air, delicious fruits, ever-
springing flowers, and wondrously fascinating and
witching scenes our American acquaintances tell us,
as we afterwards discover, with so much eloquent
exaggeration and hyperbolical truth.

But the Missionary Committee of the Methodist
Episcopal Church is in session. Let us go in; for
the doors are open to all comers, and we are deeply
interested in what is going on. Here is a large and

H

venerable gathering of Christian ministers, comprising eleven bishops, the four missionary secretaries, and a great array of living, talking intelligence, well and wisely selected from all the Conferences of the far-extending States.

Great is the importance of the work .that these men are arranging and discussing ; for the mission-fields confided to their care are almost commensurate with the world. These fields are classed under two general divisions—the Domestic and the Foreign. The interest of the Domestic Missions alone is prodigious — comprehending evangelical, educational, and, indeed, civilising work, among the weaker churches in sparse populations, the coloured people of the South, the Indians, and the Chinese ; while the Foreign Missions extend at intervals from Japan to the North-Western portions of Europe, and occupy important stations in South America and Mexico.

In this vast work the members of the Committee evidently take an absorbing interest ; and discuss with remarkable accuracy of information, keen and searching intelligence, and glowing Christian earnestness, the state and necessities of each particular Mission as it comes up in review. Each man seems to have at full command the territorial area, physical features, number of population, religious condition, and theological and other peculiarities of the field he represents ; and with a ready and, often, fervid eloquence urges its importance and claims ; while his statements and appeals are patiently heard, carefully and sympathetically examined, and im-

partially adjudicated upon by the other members of
Committee.

Such able discussions we have seldom listened to,
nor do we believe they could be excelled by any
other body of Christian ministers in the world. But
how is it there are no laymen here? It is true the
meeting is open to the public, as we think every such
meeting should be; but as the extending of the
kingdom of Christ is not committed to clerics alone,
and as clerics cannot of themselves furnish the
sinews of war, so we think they should have laymen
associated with them in the management of this great
evangelising work.

But, however this may be, the work is in good
hands—in the hands of men, who, themselves im-
pelled by the constraining love of Christ, are deter-
mined to make known this love to all for whom the
Saviour died. Nor can we refrain from admiring
their ability and zeal, wishing them God-speed, and
praying for their rapidly abounding success. But
now we must be off, and follow in the track of the
setting sun.

Having paid thirty-nine dollars and fifty cents for
a ticket to Omaha, and five dollars additional for a
berth in a sleeping-car; and having "expressed"
our baggage, we set out for the city of San Francisco.
It is eight o'clock in the evening, and our car seems
as full as it can be. Yet there is no crowding; for
each passenger has a seat for himself, upon which
none may intrude. The car itself is not inaptly
called a "Silver Palace Car;" for it is handsome

outside, while, within, its well-carpeted floor, richly-cushioned seats, double plate-glass windows that completely exclude the freezing air, mirrored sides, handsome hangings, and shining silver-plated rails, ornaments, and fittings, make it a very epitome of luxurious comfort. The berths are upper and lower, like those in a first-class steamship,—the lower being formed of what constitute the seats by day. The beds and clothes are scrupulously clean ; and everything is well attended to by a well-dressed and obliging porter, who is always at hand. At each end of the car is a neat and well-furnished lavatory,—one for ladies and another for gentlemen. Then there are two stoves which, day and night, keep up a genial temperature ; and there is an abundant supply of drinking-water kept constantly iced.

The "All aboard !" of the conductor is followed by the onward motion of the train ; and we soon leave behind us the great City robed in the darkness of night, and bespangled with innumerable gas-lights that sparkle and glimmer through the gloom.

At some distance from us—for the car is a long one—are three gentlemen, who, we are told, belong to the United States army, and who are all loudly talking about the capture of the *Virginius,* and the execution of her passengers and crew by the Cuban Spaniards. "Have you been to Washington ?" inquires one. "Yes," replies the person to whom the question is put. "Any probability of war ?" "D—n it ; I don't think so." "Have you seen Grant ?" "Yes." "Have you seen Sherman ?"

"Yes." "Well?" "Don't think there'll be any war."—"Why should there be?" interposes the third officer, who had been for a while listening in silence; and who, without waiting for a reply to his question, continues: "D—n it! The fellows went out to kill; and, instead of killing, got killed. That's the whole of it. Why should there be war?" Very sensible and epigrammatic, we think; but the blurted profanity is a conversational ornament which might with advantage have been spared. And here we cannot but observe the painful and alarming extent to which conversational profanity prevails in this land. Often and often have we been surprised and disgusted with the oaths and curses that have fallen upon our ears from gentlemanly lips. But the truth is that while in this country there is much earnest Christianity, there is also a great deal of unmasked, unblushing, and even indirectly obtrusive infidelity; which, no doubt, in a good measure accounts for the too frequent utterance by people of good social position of vulgar imprecations and oaths that seem as unbecoming the gentleman as they do the God-fearing man.

The night is spent in repose somewhat disturbed by the stopping of the train; but as the motion of the car is remarkably easy, we often, for a good while together, get fairly asleep, and we rise up in the morning a good deal refreshed.

Looking through the double glass of our window, we observe that the country is clad in "nature's winding-sheet," seeming monotonous enough, and scarcely improved by ugly stumps and arid skeleton-looking trees that protrude through the snow. At Rochester, a good "square meal," as the Americans say, for which we pay 75 cents, adds to our feeling of comfort; after which, beneath a clear sky sparkling with the rays of a full-orbed sun, we again go ahead. Evening finds us at Cleveland, Ohio, where we obtain a good dinner at a reasonable charge.

Next morning, we are curving along the margin of Lake Michigan,—a vast expanse stretching away to the horizon, undulating with foam-crested waves, and looking very like an ordinary sea. Soon we are in the famous city of Chicago, which has just risen like a phœnix from its ashes. Its inhabitants, numbering at present 400,000, seem to make merry over its late disastrous conflagration; speaking of that terrible and calamitous event as "the greatest bonfire on record." We observe that the warehouses and private dwellings, which, of course, are nearly all new, are built chiefly of brick; and we are informed that the present area of this "prodigy of the Western world" is no less than 223 square miles. But the ground upon which the city stands, as well as the country all round it, is exceedingly flat; and in its outskirts are to be seen "a considerable deal" of dirty, comfortless-looking shanties, which contrast painfully with the large and elegant domiciles that on every hand abound in their immediate vicinity.

Here, nearly 900 miles from New York, we start in earnest for "the Far West." We enter upon the prairie lands, which are as flat and uninteresting as may well be conceived; though, here and there are to be seen good houses in the midst of broad farm-lands carefully laid out and well fenced with wood. Stalks of Indian corn, from which the tops have been removed, are still standing in the fields; and patches of black soil, telling of vast supplies of coal beneath, are disagreeably conspicuous amid the half-melted snow. Rivers, lakes, and canals are all frozen, and huge spiral icicles hang from the arches of some bridges under which we pass. Night hides from us the famous Mississippi River, which we cross by a bridge, one portion of which is iron and the other wood, and altogether about a mile in length.

Next morning brings us beyond the region where snow has been falling; and, notwithstanding all the poetic praise that has been lavished on the purity and beauty of this stainless robe in which wintry Nature mantles herself, we are glad to see once more—faded and sickly though it be—the living verdure of the uncovered plain. Our fellow-travellers, mostly Americans from the Eastern States, are almost all that one could wish. One gentleman, an ex-governor of California, and lately American minister at the Court of Pekin, has a good knowledge of a former acquaintance of ours, who now occupies the high post of Inspector-General of the Imperial Customs in China, and of whom he speaks in eulogistic terms. Another, a good-natured but soft-headed

Englishman, well-fleshed, and with rather more
wit and less common sense than Anglo-Saxons
generally have, would be very amusing if he were
not often pitifully silly. But, poor fellow! though
never what one can call drunk—for he is one of
those seasoned puncheons who can hold a great
deal without rolling over—yet he has a strong
leaning towards a bottle which he alternately
empties and replenishes by the way; and, often,
at some distance from us in the car—after per-
forming antics that excite the applauding titter
and loud laughter of his immediate neighbours—
we hear him say, "Wal, oi must 'ave another
drink o' wiskey."

There is also a very thin longish East Main
man, with reddish-grey hair, small pale blue
eyes, narrow keen nose; and whose native air
seems to have made him physically arid and
shrivelled as a flower-stalk amid the frosts of
winter. This gentleman, who is going "prospect-
ing" westwards, and whom the Americans would
call "a smart man," is very anxious to please;
and, with a sharp nasal melody, intones several
anecdotes for the amusement of the company.

He is by no means sparing of the clergy, of
whom, among other cognate tales, he tells us
this:—A Southerner, wishing to spend his summer
vacation in a cooler atmosphere, visits New York.
Here he desires to hear some of the great
preachers whose fame had reached him in his
home. Accordingly, on a Sabbath morning, he

attends, in Brooklyn, the church of a minister of
uncommon preaching power. But, to his sore
disappointment, the place of the famous preacher
is on this day supplied by a minister from the
country. This stranger gives out as his text,
"But Simon's wife's mother lay sick of a fever,"
from which he preaches a "tolerable fair sermon."
In the afternoon, the Southerner attends the
church of another popular minister, whom he
expects without fail to hear. But again, he is
doomed to disappointment. For, having been seated
some time, the rustic preacher of the morning
appears, begins the service, and gives out as his
text, "But Simon's wife's mother lay sick of a
fever." The Southerner is much chagrined; but
consoles himself by resolving to attend another
church, in the evening, whose pastor is a man of
mark. Accordingly he goes. But, as it is midsummer, all the great preachers are out of town,
and so, once more, his curiosity is balked. How
is the annoyance of our Southerner intensified, when
the country substitute again shows himself, and
announces as his text, "But Simon's wife's mother
lay sick of a fever." Indeed, so disappointed and
vexed is he, that he resolves to leave New York at
once. Next morning he is seated in a railway car,
when, just before starting, who should come in but
his friend the country preacher, whom he had three
times heard the day before. Just then, some bells
are ringing in the City. "What," inquires the
minister, "is meant by the ringing of these bells?"

"Don't know," gruffly replies the Southerner, "unless that Peter's wife's mother is dead : for three times, yesterday, I heard she was sick of a fever."

At Council Bluffs, three miles east of the great Missouri river, we change our train, and pass over to Omaha, a town containing 17,000 inhabitants, and overlooking from a considerable elevation the tide below. The passage over the river is by an iron bridge, a perfect marvel of engineering enterprise and skill, and completed at a cost of one million seven hundred and fifty thousand dollars.

But how disappointed we are by the appearance of the river itself ! We have often read and thought of the great Missouri, filled with voracious alligators, fringed and shadowed with mighty forests, whose dense foliage furnished shelter for birds of curious shape and plumage, and prowling beasts of prey, and crowned with weird and romantic beauty. But what have we here ! A broad, yellow, sluggish stream, bordered with wide banks of dreary mud, and flowing through a bare, untimbered country, with scarce a sign or sound of life. Very much of what we see reminds us of Sir Walter Scott's description of another scene :

> " Nor thicket, dell, nor copse you spy
>   Where living thing concealed might lie ;
>   Nor point, retiring, hides a dell
>   Where swain or woodman lone might dwell ;
>   There's nothing left to fancy's guess —
>   You see that all is loneliness."

Yet, in this lonely place the Omahans live in apparent contentment, carrying on their business and making their dollars, and unconcerned on account of the wilderness that surrounds them. There are good hotels here, and we are glad to observe some good churches too.

At the depot here, an official—one of those "smart" men of whom we have already met a good many—looks carefully after our baggage, weighs it with such scrupulous exactness as a grocer does his tea, and very honestly charges us fifty-two additional dollars for over-weight ; though this stranger's friend well knows that he could and should forward it by a freight-train for a comparatively small sum. What an impressive and memorable illustration of what a gentleman said to us in New York—"Sir, in this country, we call a man's baggage, not the *baggage*, but—the *plunder*." Here, too, eight dollars must be paid for a berth in a sleeping-car to Ogden, and a hundred dollars for a railroad-ticket to San Francisco.

As we journey from Omaha to Ogden, we, for the first time, meet with a veritable specimen of the Indians,—a tall, upright, melancholy-looking fellow; with straight black hair, copper skin, aquiline nose, dark piercing eyes ; wrapped closely in a large blanket, and shod with some kind of untanned skin. He is looking imploringly at the passengers in the train, and willingly receives any small pieces of money, or broken bread and meat that they give.

Subsequently, we meet many of these children of

the wilderness, whose ignorance and spiritual desti-
tution cause us much pain; but whose strange
appearance and customs are curious, and sometimes
excite a reluctant smile. Many of the men, clad in
skins, and with faces painted in bars of yellow, red,
and blue, look disgustingly repulsive. The squaws,
who are generally attired in dirty coarse blankets,
are squat and strong-looking; with straight shining
black hair, broad, flattish faces, and dark cunning
eyes. The papoose, or baby, of which several of these
women have charge, is carried in a most amusing
manner. It is swathed with its back against a fiddle-
shaped board, having no part of the body exposed
except the little round swarthy face, in which are set
a pair of little twinkling, coal-black eyes. This
board, with the baby's face outward, the squaw carries
on her back, very much after the fashion in which we
have sometimes seen itinerant minstrels carry a big
violin; but, when resting, she removes the burthen
from her shoulders; and holds the fiddle-shaped
board perpendicularly in her hand, with its narrow
end, to which the baby's feet are bandaged, resting
on the ground. When a stranger gazes curiously at
the imprisoned child, the mother looks shy and half
offended, and turns sulkily away. Their dwellings,
which we sometimes see at a distance, seem very
wretched; consisting of a small tent, supported by
an upright central pole.

Many praiseworthy efforts have been made by
Christian missionaries and philanthropists, as well
as by the United States Government, to civilize,

Christianise, and save these helpless members of the human race; but it must with sorrow be admitted that, hitherto, the success of such efforts has been discouragingly small; and nation after nation of these primitive people are passing away from the soil which they once so proudly looked on as their own. Would that their future were as blessed as that expressed in the wishes and hopes of Hiawatha!

> "Come not back again to labour,
> Come not back again to suffer,
> Where the famine and the fever
> Wear the heart and waste the body.
> Soon my task will be completed,
> Soon your footsteps I shall follow
> To the islands of the Blessed,
> To the kingdom of Ponemah,
> To the Land of the Hereafter!"

But how can we rationally believe this?—since it is only they who die in the Lord that "rest from their labours;" and it is only the glorious Gospel of Christ that brings life and immortality to light.

We are now fairly in *the Far West*, running across the unbroken plains, over which the eye wanders in vain to find a human habitation—where the buffalo and antelope wander at will—where there is neither fountain, stream, tree, or song of bird—and where, like the wide expanse of ocean, the land is bounded by the far-encircling sky. What a feeling of oppressive loneliness steals like a deep shadow over the heart! How the mind recoils from solitude, and yearns for the form, the voice, and the habitation of man!

But as the still and dim evening is approaching with pensive shade, we are startled by a strange and an unexpected sight. The prairie is on fire! In front, and apparently curving round our iron path, is a circle of flame, looking almost as wide as the horizon. But it is far away ; and, as we approach, we leave it at some distance on our right hand, and so pass safely along. Such burnings, we are told, are not infrequent ; being caused sometimes by intense heat in summer, sometimes by fugitive sparks from the railway trains, and sometimes by the Indians, who, either through carelessness or by design, ignite the long dry grass of the plains.

At midnight, a soft, sweet music puts to flight unconscious sleep. What can it be ? Are we really awake ? Or do we dream ? Whence the delicious harmony that melts us, as, putting aside the curtain of our window, we gaze in vacancy and wonder upon the faintly seen plain of Nebraska, or glance upward to the heavens ? And what heavens !—so clear, so lofty, so vast—blazing with orbs marvellous in size and brilliancy, and which seem pendent from the ethereal dome.

> "—— Soft stillness and the night
> Become the touches of sweet harmony.
> Sit, Jessica : look, how the floor of heaven
> Is thick inlaid with patines of bright gold ;
> There's not the smallest orb which thou behold'st,
> But in his motion like an angel sings,
> Still quiring to the young-eyed cherubins."

But list ! The strains continue, exciting responsive emotion, almost moving us to tears. Whence come these sounds ? Are they from earth ? or is this, indeed, the fancied music of the spheres ? Presently, the harmony dies upon our ear, and silence again resumes her reign, undisturbed save by the monotonous sound of the machinery to which we are now so accustomed, and which helps to lull us to repose.

Morning brings a solution of the musical enigma of the midnight hour. What we heard was neither music in a dream nor the mystic music of the spheres, but real music, performed by a military band belonging to the United States, and which, while we were sleeping, entered the train at a fort where we stopped by the way. Kindly fellows, too, as well as good-looking, are these American bandsmen ; for, through the day, they often, for the pleasure of their fellow-travellers, awake the echoes of the wilderness with their sweetly-blending strains ; and, when they reach their destination, we see them parting from us with apparent feelings of regret.

But what a miserable thing it must be to be a soldier in the United States army. These men are, indeed, well paid, well clad, well fed, and, in appearance, would compare favourably with our smartest regulars ; but living, as they do, in the lonely frontier forts of the Far West, they are deprived of almost all the social advantages and enjoyments of civilized life.

The day is beautifully fine, and, as we push on, the Rocky Mountains come full in view. There, right before us, they lie, pile on pile, and ridge beyond ridge of massive giant elevations, lifting

their snowy peaks far up into the ethereal blue, and
sometimes hiding their huge domes within swelling
volumes of fleecy clouds.

> "Huge as the towers which builders vain
> Presumptuous piled on Shinar's plain,
> The rocky summits, split and rent,
> Form'd turret, dome, or battlement,
> Or seem'd fantastically set
> With cupola or minaret,
> Wild crests as pagod ever deck'd,
> Or mosque of eastern architect."

What an impassable barrier these mountains seem !
Yet, if we are to reach our destination, we must
pass over and through them.   And so we do.

At 3 p.m. we reach Sherman, at the lofty elevation
of nearly nine thousand feet above the level of the
sea ; having been dragged slowly up the mountain
side by two mammoth engines, that seemed to put
forth all their might in climbing the rocky steep.
Here, proudly - swelling   mounds,   sublime   peaks,
horrid depths half choked with snow, jutting and
hanging cliffs of strange and dreadful form, whose
sides are sometimes bare, and sometimes sparsely
decked with dwarfed and blasted pine and cedar ;
all impressively display the awful power of God,
and suggest ideas of wondrous geological change,
long ages, and vast internal force.

In view of a glorious sunset, we now descend at
a rapid pace, without steam, carried along by our
own momentum, and aided by the retarding force of
the air-brake ; while above, beneath, all around us,

the scenery is weirdly beautiful, and awfully sublime. Here, again, we are reminded of Scott.

> " The western waves of ebbing day
> Roll'd o'er the glen their level way;
> Each purple peak, each flinty spire,
> Was bathed in floods of living fire.
> But not a setting beam could glow
> Within the dark ravines below,
> Where twined the path in shadow hid,
> Round many a rocky pyramid,
> Shooting abruptly from the dell
> Its thunder-splintered pinnacle;
> Round many an insulated mass,
> The native bulwarks of the pass."

Arrived at the Mormon city of Ogden, a place containing about four thousand people, and forming the junction between the Union Pacific and Central Pacific Railroads, we, at a cost of six dollars, engage a berth in a sleeping-car to San Francisco. Here we part with some of our companions, who wish to visit Salt Lake City, which is thirty-six miles distant, and reached by a branch line of rail.

Having purchased a newspaper, published in Salt Lake City, we are surprised and glad to read in its columns protests and denunciations against Mormonism as strong and withering as any with which this disgusting system of filthy imposture could be anywhere assailed.

And this, it may be—though we almost doubt it—suggests the true solution of the Mormon difficulty. The so-called " City of the Saints " contains at present about twenty thousand people; but many of these

I

are what the Mormons are pleased to call Gentiles—
that is to say, Christians ; who, by means of churches,
schools, the newspaper press, and other agencies, are
exercising such an influence against Brigham Young
and his coadjutors as may ensure the ultimate and complete destruction of the Mormon religion and power.
Indeed, so potent has this influence already proved
itself to be, that one-third of the entire Mormon
population of the Territory, numbering about ninety
thousand, are said to have given up all belief in the
antichristian and demoralizing practice of polygamy,
and to have abandoned it *in toto.*

Soon after leaving Ogden, we are running along
the lonely margin of Salt Lake,—a vast expanse 150
miles long by 45 miles wide ; whose broad waters,
silent and curving shores, and skirting mountain
elevations look grey and solemn in the pale still light
of the risen moon.   Like the Dead Sea, its waters
are intensely salt and buoyant, and it seems to have
no outlet, although the Weber, Jordan, Bear, and
other rivers are continually losing themselves in its
deep, broad bosom.   In summer, evaporation considerably reduces its level, leaving immense quantities
of salt upon its uncovered rim ; yet its waters are
continually advancing on the land, and are said to be
now twelve feet higher than when the Territory was
planted first.

Night brings us through the "Great American
Desert ;" and on the morrow we pass through long
lines of snow-sheds strongly roofed with rough
planks, and through the gaping sides of which we

get sundry glimpses of Donar—a mirror-looking lake of great extent, fringed with trees and verdure; yet, in its picturesque beauty, solitary as primeval earth ere man had placed his foot upon its virgin soil.

Speeding on, we pass, by a wondrous zigzag road, our train again drawn by two powerful engines, to Summit, our highest point on the Sierra Nevadas. Here, after a good meal, which we heartily enjoyed, we begin to descend from an elevation of 7,000 feet, by a steep road, to the valley of the Sacramento. As we advance towards the lower ground, the air becomes balmy and delicious, vegetation dyed in spring-like verdure becomes abundant, human habitations multiply, and the soil is in every direction broken and furrowed by the enterprising toil of the gold-seeking miner.

But somebody shouts, "Cape Horn!" So, in a moment, the book we have been reading is dropped; and, as every one else is, we are looking through the window of our car. And what a scene! We are gliding slowly along a road scarcely wide enough to give us passage, and terraced out of the rocky shoulder of a giant cliff. On our right, the mountain rises like a perpendicular wall, lifting its towering summit to the sky; while on our left, is a rapid descent of a thousand feet to a valley, through which a river rushing seems in the distance but an insignificant silvery rill. What now if our train should leave the track, and plunge headlong through the far abyss? So it may be;

but God preserves us ; and, "the Cape doubled," we are soon beyond this amazing highway, to make which Chinamen were at first obliged, in order to get a foothold from which to work, to be let down and held by ropes from the mountain peaks above them.

Evening brings us to Sacramento, the Capital of the State of California. Of its unpaved streets, fine rows of stores and dwellings, and noble State House, surmounted by an imposing cupola, we get but a passing glimpse. Leaving this at night-fall, our attention is arrested by flames that blaze in many places in the country round us. These, we learn, are kindled by the farmers, who, in these fertile regions, have no better mode of consuming immense quantities of superfluous straw.

At night, having wound our way through the Coast Range, we find ourselves at Oakland ; which, though at the opposite side of the bay, may be regarded as a suburb of San Francisco, and reminds one of the relation of Brooklyn to the city of New York. We are soon transferred from our rolling qdarters, in which we have been so long imprisoned, to a handsome and commodious steam-boat, which in a short time lands us safely at a City wharf. A street-car brings us to a snug hotel, which we very willingly exchange for the narrow limits and ever-lasting din and motion of a railway train.

Thus, after an uninterrupted run of seven days and nights, we have passed from the Atlantic to the Pacific ; having travelled more than 3,000 miles over broad plains, through busy cities, along deep valleys, across mighty rivers, and over mountain ranges, many of whose snow-capped tops seemed like massive marble pillars supporting the azure canopy of heaven. Yet we feel little weariness, and are devoutly thankful to that kind Providence, that good and gracious God, whose tender mercies are over all His works ; and who, with a hand as loving and paternal as it is mighty, preserves the traveller as he journeys by the way.

CHAPTER X.

To see California one must not remain in the City. So, in hope of again returning to get a peep at "Frisco," let us take the rail and visit the far-famed valley of Santa Clara. Our destination is San José —pronounced San Hosé; but so clipped in its utterance by the ever-hurrying American as to make it sound like Zan-zé.

"Two dollars," says the railway clerk, as he hands us our ticket; upon which we lay down two dollar-bills,—green-backs, of course, which we have brought with us from the East. "Pooh!" exclaims the surprised official,—"What's this for? We take no green-backs here." We hand him an additional dollar-bill, telling him to charge the 10 per cent. difference between the value of our paper and gold.

This seems to have the magic power of transmuting green into yellow; but our gentlemanly clerk,—by whose ponderous gold chain, resplendent studs, and flashy rings we are almost dazzled,—kindly and honestly doubles the discount, and hands us back sixty cents as our change. This is, of course, a small affair, but it illustrates a good deal of what one may expect from smart officials in this in many ways peculiar part of the habitable globe. But our ticket paid for, we are soon on our way.

Very well-dressed people fill the cars, all of whom are good-humoured and polite. But how teasing it is to have a fellow, at frequent intervals, walking up and down between the seats, and importuning you to buy not only grapes, figs, and trashy books with showy covers, but, also, "chewing candy." Indeed, many people here seem to think that chewing is a sort of elixir of life, and that if one doesn't chew something he is almost certain to die. Perhaps there is something social in it too. For we have sometimes had a paper of tobacco handed to us, with a polite request to take a chew; and, on one occasion, when travelling in Pennsylvania, we remember to have had it said to us by a military officer that, when on duty in solitary portions of the West, he never felt lonely so long as he had a chew of tobacco in his mouth.

The view along the valley is not so charming as we thought it would be. Broad acres, with handsome trees still in leaf, there are, and, at intervals, showy houses; but beyond the immediate valley trees are few and far between, houses are scarce, solitary, and small; and the broad acres are huge bald hills, brown and withered by protracted drought. The gardens, though not without fruit-trees, vegetables, and flowers, have in general a coarse, neglected look; and seem to depend for existence upon artificial means of irrigation furnished by artesian wells, from which the water is drawn up by a windmill made of wood. But every rural scene is now at a disadvantage, as it is far advanced in November, the end of California's summer,—a summer so long, so dry, so parching, that it brings death to almost all things (trees excepted) that are not cultured by the hand of man.

But San José—fifty miles from San Francisco, and in reaching which we pass through Redwood City, San Mateo, and other new and rising towns—is really a pretty place. It contains about ten thousand people, many of whom are Romanists and Jews. Its streets,. planted with shade-trees, are laid out at right angles. It contains some pleasant squares. It has a fair supply of goodly shops. Many of its private houses give signs of wealth, and it has some excellent hotels, schools, and churches.

The Methodists have a good church here, in which we spent, with profit, some hours of a quiet Sabbath. The Presbyterians and Protestant Episcopalians are well represented here too.

A drive of three miles on the top of an omnibus, along a beautiful road, planted on each side with trees, and called "the Alameda," is really a treat. Our companions are excellent and sensible men,—one an elder of the Methodist Episcopal Church; and the other a Jewish rabbi, who has travelled much and read a great deal, but upon whose eyes there still rests the dark veil of unbelief.

These shade-trees, they tell us, were planted long years ago by Indians, the converts of Jesuit missionaries. This fact leads to some conversation on the subject of Roman Catholicism, and elicits from one of our companions the following anecdote, which, if true, illustrates the folly of assailing error by ridicule or jest.—"A Romish priest one day riding along the road was overtaken by a Protestant minister. Both were friendly, and had some pleasant chat. 'That,' said the minister, 'is not the horse on which you used to ride.' 'No,' replies the priest, 'he is dead.' 'Then,' rejoins the minister, smiling archly as he spoke, 'I suppose he is in purgatory.' 'I rather think not,' said the priest, 'I fear he is in hell.' 'Why?' asks the minister, 'what makes you think so?' 'Because,' replies the priest, 'he turned Protestant before he died.'"

At Santa Clara the Romanists have a considerable establishment, including a large chapel and a college attended by about 200 students. Here, also, the Methodists have an excellent church; and in the immediate neighbourhood they have established a university, which bids fair to exercise a commanding influence upon the rising youth of the Pacific coast.

Returning to San José, our attention is attracted by the Court House, a handsome building standing in the centre of the town. The Court is sitting, and open doors, unguarded by policeman or any such official, invite us to go in.

And so we do; admiring, as we enter, the cleanliness and comfort of the place. There are not many persons present. A trial is going on. It is a case of shooting in a saloon—one of those drinking and gambling places of which California is so full. The prosecutor is being cross-examined by a pair of lawyers, whose short and sharp interrogations are not unlike the sound of pistol-shots, and whose shrewd looks, jerking motions, and dramatic attitudes are well adapted to afford spectators fun. The Judge, a plain, fat man, without wig or gown, is seated in an easy chair, and seeming supremely indifferent to what is going on.

But behold the jurors! There they are, sitting in a double row of seats that run at right angles with the Judge's chair. Some are lolling back, as if longing to have an after-dinner nap; some are leaning forward on their elbows, looking as if unmoved either by the answers of the witness or by the quick wit and imposing gestures of his keen tormentors. But the majority of those in front have their uplifted heels resting upon the rather elevated top of the seat before them, as if calling the attention of the Court to the nails that glisten in the soles of their boots.

We are soon tired of the scene, the drama, and the actors; and, leaving the chamber of justice, we mount by a winding staircase to a tower placed on the roof of the building, from which we have a bird's-eye view of the town and of the country around it.

From San José we set out for Pescadaro, which has been represented to us as an interesting and beautiful village on the Pacific coast. But, ere we depart, winter sets in. Descending torrents deluge the lands, deep dust on the roads is changed into deeper mud, and the air, which just before was delightfully balmy, becomes chilly and raw enough to make overcoats and fires essential to comfort and health. As, however, we have railway as far as San Mateo, our journey thence is pleasant enough.

At San Mateo we, for the first time, get into an American "stage." This vehicle, drawn by four excellent horses, very much resembles a rather lengthy bread-cart on four wheels, but open in front. It is hung on strong double, treble, and even quadruple leather straps, as the nature of the roads renders the use of springs, however strong, impossible. The door is in the side, and is reached by a high step, which, in rainy weather, is covered with several inches of tough, slippery mud. Within there are four seats that run crossways, accommodating three persons each; and the floor is furnished with a covering of loose straw.

Into this machine we climb as best we can, and soon find ourselves in company with several Chinamen, who are going to the coast. Just as we are congratulating ourselves upon having the back seat, whose only other occupant is an American, an immensely fat man, who, as we afterwards learn, is an innkeeper at Spanish Town, enters the vehicle, thrusts himself wedge-like between us, and crushes us tightly against the wooden sides of the stage.

We are now full; and, as the Chinamen jabber in deep guttural tones, the driver whips his horses, and off goes our ponderous coach. In a moment or two, however, there is a heavy bump, as if the whole machine had plunged into a hole. We feel rather shaken, and our fat friend is wedged rather more fittingly into his place; but nobody expresses, or indeed, except ourselves, seems to feel, the least surprise. Soon our stage is jumping, and bounding, and plunging through a succession of puddle-holes and ruts, so as sometimes to knock our wondering head against the low roof of the machine, and occasionally to make us feel as if we had suffered dislocation of the spine. To our annoyance, while the Chinamen are alternately jabbering and laughing, our fat friend is swearing. "Why is it," we ask, reprovingly, "that so many people in this country are given to swearing?" "'Tis true, sir, 'tis true, sir, we shouldn't do it," is uttered in a half-penitent tone. And then—with wondrous self-complacence, as if he had found an ample palliation of the offence —he adds, "But we never do it in the presence of ladies." How dreadful, that men should regard even a limited observance of an express commandment of God as a matter of mere decent etiquette! Of course, we had some further talk with this misguided man, which we humbly hope may be the means to him of future good.

After a dreadful drive—dreadful, indeed, with violent shaking, rolling like the motion of a ship, thumping, plunging, and bounding—over, sometimes, very narrow and precipitous roads, with deep and splashing mud below and falling torrents above; we, at length, reach Half-moon Bay, or Spanish Town, a village at the foot of wildly beautiful, yet brown and desolate-looking mountains, and about twelve miles from where the stage set out.

In the village, inhabited by full-blooded Spaniards, Indo-Spaniards, and Americans from the Eastern States, there are some comfortable houses, with neat gardens, in which we observe a good many flowers ; and, though it is now December, there are apples on the trees. But there is nothing worth calling streets, the only substitutes for which are broad passages between short lines of houses, through which the worthy villagers wade and paddle as best they can. Of course, in the dry season these *quasi* streets are deep in dust. Here, for the first time, we observe the beautiful little humming-bird, and pay our first visit to the foam-fringed shores of the Pacific Ocean.

For, as the rain has ceased, and the sun is beaming forth from a cloudless sky, we cannot resist the impulse we feel to go yonder to the sandy beach, and touch with our hands the mighty waters of which we have so often heard and read. A walk of half a mile, through fields of stubble, without hedge or tree, and with scarcely a human habitation, brings us to the deep. There it lies before us ; not, like the Atlantic, curling and crested with foam, but gently heaving and swelling like the broad bosom of a sleeping giant; and hemmed in by the wide horizon, and by lofty cliffs and headlands that stretch dim and far away on either hand.

"Here," says Pigafetta, the biographer of the

famous Magellan—speaking of his emerging on the
28th November, 1520, from the strait since called
by his name—"we went into an open sea, while we
ran fully four thousand leagues in the Pacific sea.
This was well named Pacific, for, during the same
time, we met with no storm, and saw no land except
two small uninhabited islands, in which we found
only birds and trees. We named them the 'Unfor-
tunate Islands.' "

Stooping down, we dip our hands in the briny
tide, and feel as if we had formed a new connection,
and held a mystic and dreamy communion with a
hitherto unknown world.

But this awful stillness! This loneliness! This
conscious absence of the human! We do not, indeed,
feel what we have sometimes sung :—

> " To me 'tis one great wilderness—
> This earth without my God."

No ; for we are reverently conscious of the presence
of Him—"Which made heaven and earth, the sea,
and all that therein is." Who—

> " Bade the waves roar, the planets shine."

Yet our heart yearns for the fellowship of man ; and,
while we admire the poetry, we fail to realise the
sentiment of Byron :—

> " There is a rapture on the lonely shore,
> There is society where none intrudes,
> By the deep sea, and music in its roar."

Here, after musing for some time, we slowly retrace
our steps. To this place, to its honour be it said,

the Methodist Episcopal Church has pushed forward its advanced posts ; and a neat Methodist place of worship, with a pretty little spire, is the only church to be found either in the village or for many miles around.

But we must push on. Pescadero is our destination. So, for a further drive of sixteen miles, we again take the stage ; hoping, however, that the road may not be so bad as that over which we have been already driven, and that our bones may run no further risk of being violently jolted out of place.

Part of our wish is indeed realised ; for, *mirabile dictu,* we suffer no dislocation of joint ; but, in other respects, our disappointment is as complete as it well can be. Almost from the time we set out, the jumping, and bumping, and rocking, and rolling, and splashing, and floundering of our stage is really alarming ; often filling us with painful astonishment, as our wheels plunge into a mud-hole or strike with the suddenness of an electric concussion against the raised ends of rough timbers, which, laid horizontally, form an extemporised bridge across some deep and yawning chasm over which we are rapidly whirled.

Our way is almost entirely over lofty mountains which abut on the ocean, and along whose steep sides and sharply-jutting shoulders our scantily-terraced road runs like a thread. In many places, while on the one hand, and quite near us, the mountain rises perpendicularly above us ; on the other hand, and just outside the wheels of the stage, it runs headlong down an immense distance until it disappears in the restless wave. So that, sometimes, one is afraid of being pitched from the vehicle headlong into the deep, especially as its inner wheels are often lifted considerably while passing over clay and gravel fallen from the mountain side.

Indeed, both on this occasion and on others, we have been obliged to hold on with both hands and feet lest we should be tilted over into the sea ; or lest, while descending at a Jehu-like speed down some rugged steep, we should be shot out in front over the horses' heads. But as the horses are splendid and highly trained, and as nothing can surpass the skill of the drivers in whipping four, and, sometimes, six-in-hand along these perilous roads, serious accidents seldom happen.

At length, after sixteen formidable miles from Half-moon Bay, through mountain and ocean scenery of wondrous beauty and awful grandeur, we find ourselves in Pescadero, a small American village near the mouth of a creek, and almost entirely surrounded by hills.

Our hotel is a snug one, consisting of a series of handsome frame cottages, fronted by a long verandah, whose ornamental trellises are covered with a profusion of red and white roses intermingled with the passion-flower and the wild convolvulus. Facing the verandah is a flower-garden, watered by means of the usual wooden windmill, but, according to our ideas, not very well kept. At the opposite side of the street (if we may call it such) is a large dry-goods store, in which everything is sold at an enormous price, where the post-office is kept, and where a vigorous traffic is carried on during the whole day on Sunday. Indeed, we have often observed with pain how little the Sabbath is regarded in the country parts of California; and we have pitied as well as blamed the miserable beings who worked hard during the six days of the week, but worked harder on Sunday; giving their wretched shopmen no rest, and seeming to know no God higher than the dollar they earned, or the material advantage or sensual pleasure which it could procure.

But to return to our hotel. The establishment, like many similar ones in America, is both a hotel and a boarding-house, where a good many outsiders regularly take their meals. The proprietor is a respectable and civil man from the New England States, and everything about the concern is neat, comfortable, and admirably clean. The breakfast hour is seven in the morning, dinner is at twelve, and tea, or, more properly, supper, is at six; at which time the gong is beaten so vigorously by the muscular arm of a Chinaman that it is heard all over the village and a great way beyond it. The food is always good, abundant, and very well cooked.

There are no servants—unless, indeed, John Chinaman is pleased to accept that designation; but there are *helps*, whom we have always found to discharge their duties with efficiency and civility, but without any servility of manner.

Indeed, in this place all men are equal, as the company in the dining-room sufficiently show; for

K

here, sitting elbow to elbow, are the village trader,
the lumberer, the working mechanic, the parson, the
barber, the doctor, the stable-boy, with unpleasantly
odoriferous shoes, and the professional gambler from
the neighbouring saloon ;—all of whom have obeyed
the summoning sound of the gong, and are busily
eating and talking, without any apparent conscious-
ness of superiority or inferiority as regards intelligence, education, or rank. The only person who
seems at a social disadvantage is the Chinaman, and
"he"—to use a common Americanism—"don't
count for much." Manifestly, this pig-tailed Ce-
lestial "ain't no more thought of here than a nigger
is in the East."

One evening, as we are sitting alone in our room,
the Rev. Mr. S——, an Independent minister who
officiates in a neat church in the village, is
announced by one of the helps. Of course, we desire
the young American girl who heralds his presence
to bid him come in. So Mr. S——, a thin sharp
man, with very short dark grey hair, somewhat
wrinkled by years and climate, and attired in black
neck-tie, brownish overcoat, and pepper-and-salt
pants, is soon seated and talking at his ease.

He feels much interested in us, has been a long
time in California, knows it well, and has a dreadful
opinion of the Chinese, who are likely one day to
subvert the Government and to swamp the State.
We, in our simplicity, venture to ask him if these
Chinese do not make useful and valuable servants.
"Servants, sir ! Servants !" he exclaims, in tones

of surprise and almost angry disapproval, "Why, there are *no* servants here." We endeavour to explain what we mean. But our effort is useless. He then invites us to hear him preach ˎa very important New Year's Day sermon, which he has prepared with great care, and which will contain a great many things that will be of special advantage for us to learn,—ignorant as we are of the institutions and manners of the people among whom we have so recently come. We thank him ˎvery much, and promise to go. He then invites us to visit him in the vestry of his church, where he is at present living, for his family are in another part of the State ; and, having shaken us kindly by the hand, he bids us good-bye and retires.

We are as good as our word. Sunday finds us in Mr. S——'s church, a snug little sanctuary ; but, as most of the ungodly village community are trafficking in the stores, or drinking and gambling in the saloons, of which there are two in the place, the congregation is small.

The preliminary worship is devout and simple, after which Mr. S—— commences reading from an oldish-looking manuscript his sermon. The discourse consists chiefly of a rather bunkum laudation of America and her institutions, and vigorously exhorts the citizens of *such* a country to improve well the privileges they have. Moreover, the preacher very properly informs the people that unless they make a good use of their blessings,

these blessings are certain to be withdrawn by the
retributive providence of God. But the climax of
this somewhat interferes with our gravity. For
he adds, "If,"—and here he breaks loose from
his well-worn manuscript, raises his voice to a
shout, flourishes his arms, and looks as scathing
as lightning—"If you don't improve these blessings
as you ought, it may come to pass you'll be put
under a limited monarchy!" Here, with a furtive
glance from the corner of his eye, he observes an
involuntary smile on our face, upon which he adds,
with downcast eyelids and in a very much lowered
tone, "Ay! or under an absolute monarchy."
Soon after, the service closes, and we are not
sorry, for we have been little edified by what
we had been so urgently invited by our friend
to hear.

In this village the Methodists have a nice little
church, attended every second Sunday by a minister
from Spanish Town. As for the Protestant Episcopal
Church, it is in these regions nowhere. Neither its
places of worship, its ministers, or any other signs of
its existence come under our observation on this part
of the coast.

Passing as we are through winter, heavy rains are
the order of the day; changing the fields and hills
from sullen brown to green, and turning streets and
roads, cut out by the plough, into brimming pools
and depths of muddy slop. But fine days, with clear
sky and genial sunshine, intervene; calling forth the
song of birds, making the wooded slopes look gay,

and turning the surface of the roads into a stiff paste on which one may walk without sinking very far.

A walk of two short miles, amid wild mountain scenery, brings us to the beach. As we slowly stroll along—picking our steps, and staff in hand,—frowning crags, dark ravines, streams dotted with whistling wild-fowl, shaggy mountain-sides, and swelling hills crowned with timber are everywhere in view; but we seldom meet with man, or with a human habitation :—

> "Here, men are few,
> Scanty the hamlet, rare the lonely cot."

But we do sometimes meet a man, though never walking. For here people either drive in a wagon, with a team varying from two to six horses, or they ride on horseback. Horses, especially the mustang, a hardy Mexican breed, are abundant and cheap; and men, women, and children, canter in the saddle. Even the village barber, who charges you half a silver dollar for cutting your hair, keeps his nag and enjoys his evening ride.

Most of the few persons one meets are men, Indo-Spaniards, a race in whose veins mingle Indian and Spanish blood. Lo! here comes one just now, cantering, as usual, on his smart mustang. He wears a soft slouched hat, under which appears a round swarthy face, which a pair of full, dark, piercing eyes render sinister-looking enough. A coloured tie hangs loosely round his neck; and a light-blue overcoat, in shape not unlike those worn by British infantry, reaches far below his knees. His long heavy boots, brown and dirty, as if they had never been cleaned, are furnished with enormous silver spurs, each star-like rowel of which seems as large as a half-crown-piece. The saddle is of the old Spanish style, with high pommel, gambadoes, and broad stirrups made of wood. As he approaches, his eyes scan us with a flashing and searching glance ; and, as he passes, he greets us with a hasty salutation, and soon canters far out of sight.

And now that he has passed, not another soul is seen, nor is there a house anywhere within our view. Alone amid these mountain solitudes we wander to the shore. Stories that we have heard of grizzly bears, who are said to live at no great distance among the hills, now invade our thoughts ; and, not wishing to make such acquaintance just at present, we retrace our steps.

Indeed, we remember just now, that, one night not very long since, a grizzly in his nocturnal prowlings paid an unwelcome visit to the village and supped deliciously on a thriving pig, after which dainty repast he marched unmolested and leisurely away. Having fared so sumptuously, he was, of course, expected to return ; and so one night three brave heroes, well armed with rifles, resolved to watch his advent, and cut short at once his marauding adventures and his days. Hour after hour they waited for his coming, but they waited in vain.

At length, when tired with watching and off their guard, grizzly showed himself ; but so sudden was his appearance and so dreadful his look, that his would-be assailants were seized with panic and fled. The bear, seeing them fly, gave chase; and being too smart for one of them, seized and killed him, ere the others, recovered from their consternation, had the courage to assail and drive him off.

The remembrance of this story, combined with the awful loneliness of the place, quickens our returning steps; and we reach Pescadero just as the lusty Chinaman is summoning the boarders to supper by the loud sound of his well-beaten gong.

On a day in January, so exceptionally and exquisitely fine as to remind us of May or June when at home, we are invited by a farmer to dine with him at his dwelling up the creek. A comfortable two-horse wagon brings us, over a bad road and along a winding valley, to his house. This valley is romantically sequestered; enclosed by lofty and verdant ridges, between which a narrow crystal river meanders and eddies, reflecting from its transparent waters a sparkling and silvery sheen. The genial air is vocal with the warblings of feathered songsters, among whom we observe the blue-bird, which in size resembles the thrush, but whose plumage is an azure of exquisite hue.

On reaching the house—a neat frame cottage built on a slope facing the sun, with verandah and trellises covered with roses and creeping plants, and fronted by a neatly-kept flower-garden—we are welcomed by our bucolic friend. There is hospitable entertainment for us too; for on the table we have mildly-cured pork, salmon, butter, honey, cheese, pickles, bread, potatoes, apples, pears, confectionery, and tea ; all of which, except the last, have been raised on the farm, and afford us an ample and delicious meal.

Subsequently, our host conducts us through his fields, many of which are studded with great squashes, upon which well-fed cattle regale themselves at will. He shows us where such a sweeping torrent as Californian rains can yield, descending lately from the mountains, carried with it, in its headlong course, embankments, trees, huge boulders, and even large patches of cultivated land. He points out to us blackberries carefully cultivated, and propped with upright stakes, and which, he tells us, make an excellent jam.

Then, here are his outhouses—large wooden sheds, with lofts—in which are stores of fine potatoes, popcorn, pears, apples, and other products of the farm ; at which our host looks thoughtfully, shakes his head, and says, " We have abundance of these things, but we can get *no* money ; everything is plenty here, except money." He then informs us that the towns are so distant, and the roads so bad, and the prices so low, that it wouldn't pay him to carry his produce to market. And so, again, he adds, with a desponding shake of the head, "*No* money ; *no* money : we can get *every*thing here but *money !* " Our first impulse is to laugh at the lachrymose tone, drooping lids, and elongated visage of our lugubrious friend ; but when we think that these products of the field and garden are perishable and perishing ; that, in other circumstances, they might be exchanged for cash ; and that this again might be exchanged for clothes, furniture, utensils, and other equally valuable and needful things, we feel there is some ground for regret, if not for desponding complaint.

Rumbling and jolting homeward in our wagon towards nightfall, as the pale light of the full-rounded moon mingles with the grey shadows of the encircling hills, our ears are assailed by what seems the loud and sharp whistling of innumerable wild-fowl. "What birds are these?" we inquire from the farmer's son, an intelligent young man, who sits beside us holding the reins of his tugging and floundering team. "Birds! Birds! Ha, ha, ha! Birds, indeed! These are not birds ; they are *frogs.*" And so we found out afterwards they really were. And here, let us add that both in this place and in other parts of America, the shrill and uproarious noise caused by the nightly revels of these hideous creatures has often fairly filled us with surprise. Can it be that Americans anywhere eat these dreadful things? We have heard of their doing so in some places ; but we have never seen it, and we seriously doubt it. At any rate, it must be,—that is, if done at all,—an eccentric stomach that can find delight in digesting legs and shoulders of these loud-whistling and half-screaming tenants of the pond and pool.

As we enter the village we pass the door of a large

hotel. But it is entirely shut up, and, although in good order, it has a sinister and forsaken look. On inquiry, we find that its proprietor and several members of his family are in San Francisco gaol, awaiting their trial for the dreadful crime of murder. Some months ago these people, who had been previously regarded as respectable, in a scuffle with a neighbouring family about the possession of a homestead, used firearms foully and freely, and shot one of their opponents dead; which so roused the indignation of the villagers and the people scattered over the adjoining lands that they resolved to lynch them; and would have done so, but for the timely appearance of the sheriff, who rescued them from a summary trial and a speedily-executed death.

This lynch-law is a dreadful thing. And yet, we fear that the lawlessness and violence prevalent in some parts of the Western States have sometimes made it needful for the protection of human life. For one cannot help asking, how is society to exist in places where magistrates are either too corrupt or too cowardly to execute the laws; and where organized and red-handed ruffianism is a terror and a danger to the orderly and well-disposed of every class? But as soon as society becomes more settled and better ordered, and as soon as the laws become equitably and vigorously administered in these remote places, we believe the summary and sanguinary functions of Judge Lynch will altogether cease.

The time having come when we must leave the rural parts of California, we do so without any feeling of regret. People accustomed to the rigorous winters and scorching summers of New England, or to the fever-and-ague-breeding heat of the Southern States, may honestly boast of its wonderful climate ; but, taking the climate of California all the year round—with its long and withering drought in summer and its drenching rains in winter—we do not believe it is to be compared to the climate of the British Islands.

Moreover, we are persuaded that the fertility of California, which in some places is certainly great, is not so much the result of its atmosphere as it is of the marvellous depth and richness of its soil. For, in some of the valleys especially, it is surprising to what a depth one can dig ; and the subsoil, however remote from the surface, is as rich and prolific as that on the top.

As might be expected in a country so new and remote, and so sparsely populated with a medley of cosmopolitan adventurers, society is found wanting, even when tried by the ordinary standards of civilized life. We have, indeed, met some excellent Christian people here, and not a few who are even refined ; but, in general, society is low, vulgar, profane, and morally loose. Professional gamblers and vilest drinking saloons are to be found in the smallest villages ; and the principal amusement is dancing, accompanied with rough freedoms, and often followed by immoral results. Wanton and shameful divorce, with its hideous antecedents, concomitants, and results is a great deal too common ; and here, as in other parts of America, is too readily sanctioned by the accommodating laws of the State. And while the American people, notwithstanding their many excellent qualities, seem naturally irreverent,— having, *in general,* scant veneration for parents, pastors, magistrates, places of worship, and, in very many instances, for God Himself; there is, *as a rule,* the least possible respect in the minds and manners of the levelling Californians for things human and divine. There is an off-hand liberality, a hospitality, and seemingly generous way of doing business that one cannot but admire ; but, with all this, there is, on the part of too many, a great deal of shrewd, fox-like scheming, that smiles while it cheats you, and exultingly laughs when it believes you undone.

But we must not forget that things here are better than they were. Indeed, in many respects there is a vast improvement in a short time ; and when, with an increase of population, of agricultural and commercial enterprise, and of education in this vast and fertile region, there is also an increase of that "pure and undefiled religion" which springs from the gospel of Christ, and from the Spirit of God, we are persuaded that California will be in every respect— "As the garden of the Lord."

CHAPTER XI.

It is eight in the morning as we stow ourselves into the stage. Though it is not raining, the clouds are disagreeably ominous, mists hang upon the hills, and a chilly moisture permeates the air. Bidding good-bye to a few recently-made acquaintances, the horses plunge forward through the flying mud ; and, with Pescadero behind us, we are soon rolling, rocking, and bumping along the narrow and deep-rutted road that leads to San Francisco. Avoiding Spanish Town and San Mateo, our way is through Redwood Valley to where we are to find the railroad at Redwood City.

A lady-passenger, taken up at an inn by the way, keeps up a smart conversation with the driver, to whom she complains much of Chinese servants ; saying, amongst other things equally feminine and elegant,—"They ain't no good whatever, unless they are knocked down every day."

Having mounted a long succession of hills, we descend into the valley by a precipitous slope, when the clouds give ample fulfilment of their promise in the morning ; and soon every gaping chink of our rocking and jumping vehicle becomes a jet, through which a powerful and blustering wind drives in upon

us a watery stream.   Lofty and wide-spreading trees
also furnish an aqueous contribution ; for they sometimes shake down upon us copious accumulations of
drops gathered by their ample foliage from the bursting clouds, giving us a good idea of how the rains
of the Deluge must have beaten against the roof and
sides of Noah's Ark.

Yet, amid all our discomfort, we cannot help
admiring the graceful sweep of the ever-bending
valley, its thickly-wooded sides, and, above all, the
towering grandeur and majestic beauty of many of
its trees.   Most of these trees are what the Californians call *redwood*, and seem to be a species
between the cedar and the pine, and to combine the
qualities of both.

Leaving the valley, by a slow and laborious progress we reach the summit of a lofty mountain ; but
mists intervene between us and what, in a clearer
atmosphere, would be a wonderful expanse of view.
But shall we ever forget our descent from this
towering elevation to Redwood City ! The mountain
side is long, steep, and rugged ; the fine horses are
powerful and fiery ; the driver, a large, athletic man,
has a daring equalled only by his wondrous skill ;
time has been lost by the wind and rain and by the
injured condition of the roads ; and the last train
for "Frisco" is likely to be missed.

Now the driver is excited, the foaming steeds
slashed, and the flying stage—amid lumps of mud
that shoot around us like a ceaseless shower of
meteors—sometimes hopping, sometimes tilting over

at a fearful angle, sometimes jumping as if lifted from all its wheels at once, comes whirling down a descent of four awful miles towards the plain.

Here we are, holding on with hands and feet, fearing the worst, hoping the best, wondering how it will end, praying we may not be killed, and sometimes involuntarily smiling at a plump little woman in the seat before us, who is holding fast with all her might, and alternately uttering cries of fear and bursting into fits of loud, hysterical laughter.

At length, by the good providence of God, we are safely in the plain, and soon after we are quietly seated in the train on our way to the city. Night brings us to San Francisco, where we are most kindly received and hospitably entertained by a noble-hearted Hibernian, in whose house and with whose family we for some weeks after find a quiet and comfortable Christian home.

The appearance of San Francisco is imposing and picturesque. Rising up from the magnificent bay, whose wooden wharves are crowded with shipping, its buildings cover a wide area, much of which ascends in steep elevations, and was, till very recently, a series of unsightly sand-hills. The principal business streets are wide, with good shops and showy offices; and a restless-looking, motley throng, collected from almost all the nations of the world, are hurriedly moving to and fro along the busy ways. Other parts of the city are quiet-looking enough. Most of the private houses are wood, with flights of steps in front, bay windows, balconies, and verandahs;

all of which are elaborately ornamented and bright with paint. Churches of all denominations shoot up their spires against the sky, and a few of the hotels are imposing in their elegance and size.

But most of the streets, with side-walks of plank, are wretchedly paved; and the crossings, which are ever presenting themselves at the ends of the blocks, are apt illustrations of "the Slough of Despond." The atmosphere, in many places, is unpleasantly odoriferous with greasy smells, emanating from numerous restaurants—high, low, cheap, middling and dear—which on every hand abound.

To the eye of a stranger, the most striking figure in the streets is the Chinaman, with his swarthy skin and oval dark eyes, quietly moving about-in blue tunic, broad trousers, and thick-soled slippers, while his black and neatly-braided pigtail hangs from his pole almost to his heels. Of the 200,000 inhabitants of San Francisco, we are told 25,000 are Chinese, some of whom are merchants, others small traders and mechanics, but the great mass of whom are labourers and domestic servants. In this last capacity we have observed many in white tunics, some of whom are boys little older than children, and who are discharging all the duties usually allotted to a housemaid. Many of these people also keep laundries, and are famous for the elegant make-up of the linen which they wash.

But the Chinese never make America their home. They come simply to gather up a certain number of dollars, and when this is accomplished they return to

their native land again. And should any of them
die, their remains are transmitted for burial to China,
which they regard with some such feelings of veneration and love as those with which the Israelite regards
the Holy Land.

It is deplorable to think that these people, bringing
with them their heathen superstitions, set up in many
places their "Joss House," or heathen temple, and
practise their idol worship in the midst of a professedly Christian nation. Yes, and in this worship,
so degrading, demoralizing, and impious, they are
carefully protected by "the powers that be;" for
we remember, when in San José, the Chinese Joss
having been surreptitiously taken from his house, the
police were sent on a special mission to hunt out and
bring back the stolen god.

But we are told this is LIBERTY. Indeed! Then,
if so, Liberty is suicidal; for it takes from a professedly Christian State the sacred right of protecting
itself,—of protecting itself against worse than an
armed enemy,—against a most baleful moral and
social abomination. Besides, it is absurd and stulti-
fying for a nation to shut and carefully guard her
ports against the ingress of plague-stricken immi-
grants; and yet to open them wide to infernal idola-
try, with its impious rites and morally and socially
ruinous results. It is high time, we think, for
Christian America to remember that there are limits
to political freedom; that Liberty ought not to be
permitted, Saturn-like, to devour her own offspring;
and that she who, at so terrible a cost, swept negro

L

slavery from her soil, should—crushing twin dragons
in the birth—deal promptly, firmly, and vigorously
both with Mormon polygamy and with the legalized
worship of idol gods.

Some of the Chinese, however, have turned from
dumb idols to the living and true God ; and we have
had the pleasure of visiting the Mission premises of
the Methodist Episcopal Church, where a goodly
number of these interesting people are receiving both
secular and religious instruction ; some of whom, by
their pious and exemplary lives, are living witnesses
of the power of Jesus to save men not only from
degrading error, but also from sin.

But the state of society in this city strikes us as
being singularly strange. There is much comfort,
wealth, refinement, and even elegance, combined with
savage violence and frequent bloodshed. Murders
and suicides are of common occurrence ; and, during
our stay of a few weeks, we have been often amazed
at the vile and ruffianly scurrility vented and vended
through the daily press. We have been startled,
too, by a pair of editors, who have attempted to
settle their quarrels by deliberately pistolling each
other in the open day, and in one of the principal
streets. Indeed, it is hard to say when one, however inoffensive, is perfectly safe ; for we have known
the case of a lady, who, while quietly purchasing
some goods in a shop, was wounded by a ball from
the street, which one *gentleman* thought fit to fire
at the head of another.

Even some of the gentler sex themselves can

utilize the deadly revolver, and do an assassin's work ; of which the following occurrence, that took place some time after we left, and which we copy from a reliable daily paper, will furnish an illustrative proof :—" Some little excitement was caused at San Francisco on the morning of the 23rd of December, owing to General Moses G. Cobb, a leading lawyer of the city, being shot in Washington-street by a veiled assassin. The learned gentleman was walking down the street arm-in-arm with a friend, when a woman, whose face was covered with an old brown veil, shot him in the back with a revolver. He immediately fell, and, being picked up by Judge Botts and a few friends who happened to be near at the time, was conveyed to an adjacent store. He was subsequently taken to his home, and, by latest accounts, there is a fair prospect of his recovery. In the meantime, the veiled assassin surrendered herself and her pistol to a police-officer, and turned out to be Mrs. Hannah Smythe, who was dissatisfied with the manner in which General Cobb had conducted a lawsuit on her behalf. On being taken into custody, she expressed no contrition for her deed, but, on the contrary, appeared to be in capital spirits, and laughed at the idea of ' mitigating circumstances.' When it was suggested to her that a plea in palliation of the crime she had committed would probably help her with the jury, she jocosely remarked, with a grin, that she cared no more for her life than for one of the old shoes on her feet. Her appearance is more striking than pleasant. Her face is colourless and without expression. She has a broad, flat forehead, prominent cheek-bones, a large mouth, with thin, vindictive lips, and a chin square cut and of masculine firmness. She is very abusive in her language, and altogether is not a prepossessing person."

In San Francisco faithful ministers of the Gospel are not wanting; nor do we fail to find many men and women in the membership of the churches of high Christian character, large liberality, and exemplary zeal. Yet, many of the clergy whom we have heard are poor expositors of Scripture, and a good deal given to clap-trap oratory, now and again interlarded with vulgar wit. Indeed, with rare exceptions, here, as in the East, Scripture exegesis seems at a discount; and a few of the expositions at which we have wondered, and by which our ears have been pained, have been marvellous specimens of ingenious ignorance. Yet, there is much heartiness, much zeal; and often, especially in conducting protracted religious meetings, which, happily, are not confined to any one religious denomination, there is much success in bringing sinners to God.

But what would Old-Country folks think of this? It is Sunday evening, and Mr. L——, a popular Presbyterian minister, is to preach. The sermon s to be a controversial reply to a Roman Catholic priest, who has made an absurd onslaught upon Protestant Missions. We find our way to the church, a spacious and beautiful building, and crowded in every part. Mr. L—— reads his defence of Protestant

Missions with much animation, at the close of which
he breaks forth in extemporaneous triumph, exclaiming :—"And now I have done ! But let father C——
remember, I have *not* done with *him !* I have only
made a *beginning !* I have fired off only *one* barrel
of my revolver ! *Five* other chambers are loaded ;
and, when occasion requires, I am ready to discharge
them !"—a defiant and fiery peroration which the
audience received with roaring laughter and a pretty
general clapping of hands.

But a scene more marvellous to us takes place
in the course of the week. " Will you come to
the concert to night?" invitingly inquires a friend.
We express our thanks, but answer, " No." He
then informs us that it is to be in M—— Street
Presbyterian Church—not, however, the one of which
we have already spoken—and, moreover, that it is
to be "for the *benefit* of the church." Well, then,
of course, it is to be a sacred concert ; and, as our
friend has purchased several tickets at a dollar
apiece, we shall accept one and go. Yet, if we
had not, some time before, when in a town in New
Jersey, heard it announced to a Methodist congregation, on a Sunday morning, that during the following
week there were to be two sacred concerts "held in
the church for the benefit of the Sunday-school,"
the thing would have had an outlandish sound in
our ears.

Evening finds us in the church, where, as we
enter, we are presented with a printed programme
of the concert. In the centre of the building, which

is really a fine one, is a raised platform, upon which stands a massive piano. There may be 1500 people present; amongst whom is the reverend Pastor, who, seated in front of one of the side galleries, seems viewing the audience and watching the proceedings with considerable zest.

We glance at our "Programme," but there is nothing sacred here; secular songs, such as "The Last Rose of Summer," and pianoforte solos constitute the whole. Madame B——, a celebrated *prima donna*, and several others, sing for the amusement of the audience; and Mr. C——, who, we believe, is a professional musician, renders with skill and taste several musical compositions on the grand piano. There are a good many *encores*, with the usual applause; and so ends the "Concert for the Benefit of the Presbyterian Church." Shade of Knox! Spirits of the old Covenanters! What think ye of this? Is this the religious freedom for which ye fought and bled?—Methinks myriads of Presbyterian voices on earth, and myriads more in heaven, emphatically thunder forth an indignant No!!!

As time rolls on, we are anxious to witness the services in a Protestant Episcopal Church. Here is one of good architectural pretensions, so we shall go in and join in the worship which is just now about to commence. We like the prayers, the repetition of the creeds, and the reverential reading of the Scriptures. There is much singing, too; all of which is lively and good. The text is

a fine one, brimming over with evangelical truth.
But what a miserable sermon! The clergyman,
who delivers himself in white, surplice, reads with
good elocution of voice and manner a well-got-up
composition. But there is little or nothing in it
to save,—little or nothing of Christ in His great
atoning work,—little or nothing to grapple with
the conscience of the sinner, to heal the broken-
hearted, or to help the saint in his upward struggle
towards the Kingdom of God. Never before have
we been so impressed with the value of a Scriptural
liturgy; for, without it, how little of divine truth
would these people have to feed upon to-day! The
gentleman in white, with his twenty-minute rhetorical
declamation, may be very correct, very polished,
very pleasing; but we fear, if what we have heard
be a sample of his usual evangel, he must by his
preaching, however else he may effect it, fail to
fulfil his mission to the people,—"To open their
eyes, and to turn them from darkness to light,
that they may receive forgiveness of sins, and
inheritance among them that are sanctified by faith
that is in " Christ.

We are not aware whether there are ritualistic
tendencies here or not. We rather think not. But
we have met with them in other parts of America,
though we have not seen them developed in any
very startling degree. Nor do we believe that such
tendencies, however fostered by a would-be sacerdotal
section of the clergy, can ever find much favour with
the generality of the American people.

We remember on one occasion being much impressed with this thought. In a considerable town in one of the Eastern States, we, on a *holiday*, entered a Protestant Episcopal Church where divine service was being celebrated in due form. The clergyman, a good-looking man, whose large jetty whiskers contrasted strongly with his snowy robe, was reading the service in fine solemn tones and with admirable accent; but his only auditors were two ladies, besides the person who assisted by answering the responses. Whether these holiday-keeping ladies were members of the clergyman's family or not we had no opportunity of knowing, but we strongly suspect they were.

The return of the Sabbath brings us to C—— Methodist Episcopal Church. Not much fear of ritualism here. The place looks well, but is not very large; and, although there are no galleries, there is plenty of unoccupied room. The sermon is much more expository and less sensational than sermons here usually are; but it is so cold, so arid, so devoid of unction and power, as to remind us of a sapless skeleton that lies bleaching in the frost.

But how painful it is to observe that the authorised Methodist Hymn-book, a noble collection of songs for the sanctuary, seems not to be used by the Methodist churches here. It is superseded by a compilation prepared by a person who has neither the poetic nor the literary qualifications for so important and difficult a work; and who, by ill-judged liberties, has, in some instances, marred the theology, the poetry, and even the grammar of some of the finest lyrics that have ever been composed for the worship of God. How surprised, and almost vexed, we are, when, at the close of this service on the forenoon of the Sabbath day, the hymn is given out commencing with :—

> " There's a light in the window for thee, brother,
>   There's a light in the window for thee :
> A dear one has gone to the mansions above,
>   There's a light in the window for thee.
>   A mansion in heaven we see,
>   A light in the window for thee ;
>   A mansion in heaven we see,
>   And a light in the window for thee."

This sort of thing seems almost a burlesque of the solemnities of public worship ; and could scarcely be excused, even if the Pastor of the church had been preaching the funeral sermon of some departed member of his flock.

Our afternoon is agreeably spent in the Sunday-school of the H—— Street Methodist Episcopal Church. The school-room is large, handsome, and well-furnished. About 600 children of all ages are present, under the instruction of a good staff of teachers, and everything is working harmoniously and efficiently under the able superintendence of our excellent Hibernian friend. In the same church we have a good sermon from the Pastor in the evening, followed by a prayer-meeting, in which there is deep earnestness, with occasional outbursts of hallowed enthusiastic fire.

Female agency is much more used in the American churches than in ours, and with very great advantage, we think. Often, when we have seen American women forming themselves into committees for visiting and relieving the sick and poor, for looking after the comforts and supplying the wants of the parsonage, for getting up Sunday-school festivals, and for many other "good works for necessary uses ;" and when we have witnessed the hard work of even mothers of families in connection with Dorcas, tract, and other benevolent societies ;—we could not but think their conduct worthy of imitation by not a few. of the female members of our churches at home, who, *because it is not* THEIR *business,* never ask if there are any sick and poor to be looked after, whether the minister's residence is commonly comfortable and decent or not, or whether the Sunday-school is living or dead. In praise of the hearty practical interest which many excellent lady-members take in the affairs of our churches, we cannot say too much ; but we are persuaded their number is small compared with what it might be, and compared with the large amount of female talent, energy, and influence that fail to be utilized, and that accomplish nothing, or next to nothing, for Christ and His cause.

But it is a question whether, in some respects and by some parties in America, the notion of female agency in the churches is not pushed a little too far.

Just now a protracted meeting, which, as we have already explained, means a series of revival services, is being held in P—— Street Church. The person

who conducts these services is a lady who feels herself divinely called, and, for aught we can tell, truly
so called, to this kind of work. We visit the church,
where a large number of people are gathered.
Mrs. ———, a round-faced, amiable-looking woman,
tall, stout, and broad-shouldered, rises to preach ;
while just behind her sits the Pastor of the church,
an Americanized Englishman of no great physical
bulk.

The discourse is intrinsically poor ; but it is
delivered with such earnestness, and with such
vigorous yet graceful, indeed we may say dramatic,
gesture as we have seldom, if ever, seen surpassed.
In truth, our lady-preacher seems an ecclesiastical
Penthesilea, doing mighty battle against the combined
forces of the devil and sin. But of the perfect ortho-
doxy of her theology we are more than in doubt.
For, in addressing her hearers, she says,—"If there
be *any* sin in you ; if it has not been *all* cast out, *all*
destroyed ; you have NEVER been converted AT ALL."
—And then, turning round and looking the Pastor
straight in the face, she, with great vehemence,
and in deep contralto tones, interrogates him thus :—

Mrs. ———. "Is it not so ?"

Pastor makes no answer.

Mrs. ———. "I *say*, is it not so ?"

Pastor is silent.

Mrs. ———. "I say, *is* it not *so ?* Is not *such* the
fact ? *Answer* me. *Answer* me ! I say."

Pastor, looking nonplussed and a little bit be-
wildered, is still silent.

Mrs. ——, taking silence for consent, and gesticulating with all the flourish and air of a triumphant orator, exclaims,—"Ah! Ah! I knew it was *so!* I *knew* it was so!"

The sermon over, Mrs. ——, marshalling to her aid a goodly number of praying men, commences a meeting for prayer, singing revival hymns, exhortation, and relating religious experience; in the course of which she sometimes exhorts, sometimes marches up and down the aisles warning and encouraging the people, and sometimes raises a hymn accompanied by the loud and rhythmical clapping of her hands. She permits no pause in the proceedings, except for the purpose of relating religious experience; for if at other times an interval of silence should occur, she immediately cries out,—"Let *another* brother pray," or, "*Sing* on, brethren; sing *on*."

Much of this is not quite to our taste; yet we dare not say anything against it, lest in disparaging the chaff we should also undervalue the wheat. For, manifestly, a good work is going on; careless people are stirred up on the subject of religion, and not a few, who have been hitherto very ungodly, profess to have been turned to the Lord.

But, some days after, certain utterances at a meeting of ministers are as startling as they are novel. The attendance is good, and the subject under discussion is this:—"Ought women to be *ordained as pastors* of churches?"—A good many are decidedly on the negative side; but there is also a strong array of affirmatives. One brother sees no reason whatever why women should not be regularly ordained to the pastoral office as well as men ; but, on the contrary, thinks it very desirable. For his own part, he thinks a woman might even be made a bishop, and, if it were so, he should not be sorry to receive ordination at her hands.

A stranger present is asked by the chairman what he thinks. To which he replies that his education, prejudices, feelings, and convictions are all against any such thing ; and expresses his regret that the advocates of this measure have not endeavoured to argue their case from the standpoint of Scripture.

This arouses an excellent and intelligent man on the other side, who, looking pale with excitement, starts to his feet and commences a spirited harangue in favour of women's rights in general, and of their right to the Christian pastorate in particular. Amongst other things, he declares that he recognizes no difference between man and woman, save that the one wears one kind of garment, and the other another. "And now,"—he adds,—"as for Scripture, is it not written,—'So God created *man* in His own image, in the image of God created He him ; *male* and *female* created He THEM !' Is not this equality ?—*perfect* equality ?—equality in *all* things ?"—"Read on farther," interlocutes the stranger,—"'And *He* shall *rule* over *thee*.'"—This is like the sudden discharge of a pistol-shot, which so disconcerts the good man that he becomes still more excited, looks a whiter pale, stammers and sputters, begins to rate

the stranger soundly, because that he, a subject of
Queen Victoria, should hold so unbecoming an
opinion ; and, finally,—seeming to have lost the
thread of his discourse, and to be very hard up for
either thoughts or words to express them,—amid the
merriment of the meeting, and with a rocking, rolling
motion, like a ship righting herself after being struck
by a heavy sea, he settles down upon his seat. Finally,
this question, like many other questions, was settled
by being left as it was.

A visit to the public schools here convinces us they
are good. They are not unlike the Model National
Schools in Ireland ; only they are chiefly taught by
women, who have neither assistant teachers nor
monitors. Indeed, the Lincoln schools, in which is
taught, besides English in all its branches, music,
drawing, and modern languages, and which contain
about 1200 pupils of all ages and of both sexes, seem
an aggregate of small schools brought together in the
same building ; for each teacher has a school-room to
himself or herself with about 50 pupils, to whom he
or she teaches everything, without any kind of help
or any division of labour. And upon this anti-Lan-
castrian principle, we are told, the public schools in
America are generally conducted. They are supported
by a tax which the citizens levy upon themselves,
and all the pupils who attend them go free.

The public markets are a wonder. They contain
all that is edible of flesh, fish, and fowl ; and, though
it is now the depth of winter, they are plentifully
supplied with green peas, asparagus, and, in short,

almost every variety of spring vegetable and summer fruit. But Californian mutton, though very abundant, had better for the most part be eschewed than chewed ; for, when between the teeth, it might pass for boiled gutta-percha. Much of the beef is uncommonly fine. Such products, however, as veracious lecturers in the Eastern States have told us of, we have not been able anywhere to find. We have not seen " squashes as big as American flour-barrels," nor "a cabbage so large that a man at noonday might stretch himself at full length under its shade."

But how vexatious it is to hear everybody saying, this is the finest and most agreeable season of the year. Fine days there certainly are, with bright sunshine and genial air ; but, as a rule, the morning atmosphere is chill with light hoar frost, the rain pours down in torrents during the greater part of the day, and the streets everywhere, save on the plank, or on the few flagged side-walks, are deep in mud.

Then, you are told, there is no summer evening in San Francisco. The summer mornings, people say, are beautifully fine ; but about 11 a.m. it blows a gale, driving heavenward a perpetual cloud of sandy dust that sometimes beats like snow-flakes against the obscured window-panes. This gale falls about 5 p.m., when a heavy fog sets in from the Pacific, blinding the sky and mantling the landscape in a dismal grey.

Earthquakes, too, are not infrequent ;—splitting walls, toppling chimneys, making all the delf clatter in the pantries, pitching women down the stairs, and, without notice or ceremony, tumbling unthinking people from their windows head foremost to the streets. Happily, we ourselves have not experienced such unpleasant movements of *terra firma;* though we have been told in San Francisco, that there really was an earthquake on the day we travelled from Pescadero to the City. But on that day we got such a woful shaking in the stage as must have effectually prevented our feeling any vibrations or undulations of the agitated earth.

CHAPTER XII.

TROY.

A DARK morning, with steady bath-like showers, sees us taking leave of San Francisco, for the purpose of again pushing eastward over mountain, river, and wide-extending plain. The journey is accomplished as before described, save that this time we pass through about 200 miles of the Canadian Dominion. To our eye Canada seems not nearly equal to the States either in the size and arrangement of its towns, the wealth of its people, or the build and neatness of its homes. But our observation of these matters is of necessity very limited, and we are not in a position to make any just estimate of the comparative merits of these neighbouring lands.

For the present our stay is at Troy, a smart, well-built city on the Hudson river, about 150 miles from New York, and six miles from Albany, the capital of the State. It contains about 50,000 people, many of whom find amply remunerative employment in extensive ironworks, and in the manufacture of woollen, cotton, and other kinds of useful goods.

Here we find another noble specimen from the Emerald Isle, whose upright character, godly zeal, and able ministrations render him a pillar and an ornament to the Church of which he is a minister.

M

From this excellent man and his estimable family we receive a fraternal welcome and a generous hospitality while we stay. He has two brothers in the ministry, one of whom it was our happiness to know in New York, and of whose attention and kindness we have a fragrant recollection.

In this city there are many handsome and commodious churches, some of the finest of which belong to the Methodists. But, as we enter one of the most beautiful of these edifices, how painful it is to see some such notice as this appended to its inner doors :—" Please don't spit on the carpets of this church."

We are informed that the winter is a mild one,— remarkably mild. Yet the broad and deep Hudson is frozen into crystal masses of ice, and the country all round is wrapped in a perpetual winding-sheet of snow. Sometimes the winds are really furious ; obliging the brave Trojans to muffle their noses as closely as possible; lest, peradventure, this important and prominent functionary of the human face should be denuded of its skin by the fierce assaults of the Boreal blast. But, generally, by day the sky is clear, the sun bright, and the air bracing, and even exhilarating ; leading one to prefer an outdoor walk to the dull atmosphere of an over-heated room.

For some weeks revival services are held in several churches, at some of which there is rather much of what borders on ranting and hysterical excitement ; yet they are the means of bringing many sinners within the toils of the Gospel net ; and, at a very interesting and solemn service, we have the pleasure of witnessing the formal reception of several members into the Church; persons who by means of these special meetings have been brought to a saving knowledge of the Lord.

Here, for the first time in our life, we witness "a golden wedding." A gentleman and his wife who have been married fifty years are met by their friends; congratulated, and complimented, and presented with a silver salver well filled with dollars of shining gold. Silver weddings, too, we are informed, are common; and so are weddings of tin and weddings of wood. In the last case, we learn that sundry wooden bowls, washing-tubs, buckets, and such like, are formally presented to the happy pair, whose wooden wedding is celebrated by themselves and their friends. But whether the wedding should be gold or silver, tin or wood, does not depend upon the rank of those to whom the gifts are presented, but upon the number of years they have been associated in matrimonial bonds; the wood, tin, silver, and gold indicating a graduated scale of years of married life. Of course, the lowest number is indicated by the wood, and the highest by the gold.

A ministerial meeting gives us an opportunity of hearing a theological discussion. A minister who fears that some of his countrymen are making too much of what is called "the higher life," to the disparagement of a state of justification, has read a sermon in which, according to the judgment of some, he has too highly extolled the condition of a justified man. Passages from Wesley's sermons are quoted against what has been read. To which some on the opposite side reply that, in these passages, John Wesley contradicts himself. A person present remarks that this is unlikely, inasmuch as Mr. Wesley was a famous logician ; and that the passages quoted are all taken from the first fifty-three sermons, which he himself revised with scrupulous care, and which are now used as doctrinal standards by his followers in England. " Have you," inquires a minister present, turning to the minister whose sermon is being discussed, but evidently intending his remark for those on the opposing side, "read Tyerman's Life of Wesley ? " " No ; " is the brief and prompt reply. " Then,"—rejoins his friend,— " get it, and read it ; and, when you do, you will form a much lower estimate of the authority of Wesley and his opinions than you have hitherto had." To this no one makes reply ; and we, who have not read Mr. Tyerman's volumes, wonder if this thing can be true ?

One of those present is a German minister, whose conversion, we are told, took place as follows. He was "down South " some years ago, and attended a meeting where all but himself were jetty black. He was deeply convinced of sin, and cried aloud in keen anguish of soul. All the darkies, men and women, have prayed for him in turn, except a little negro girl in the company, who is thought too young to engage in audible intercessory prayer. The German continuing unhappy, the poor dark child implores with streaming eyes that she also might be permitted to offer her petitions in his behalf. Consent is given; and, as this dear child-in-bonds breathes forth her desires in the name of Jesus at the Mercy-seat, the distressed penitent is able to trust fully in the merit of the Saviour, and finds peace with God through believing. What say some of our anthropological philosophers to this FACT? Well; it matters not what they say; we know what is written,—"Out of the mouths of babes and sucklings hast thou ordained strength."

Our stay in Troy gives us an opportunity of attending several of what our American friends call "Sociables." Now, the idea of a sociable is good. It is to gather the members of the church together, for the purpose of having a little agreeable and profitable social intercourse, and of strengthening those bonds of union which should always exist between members of the same congregation. And, in many instances, they, no doubt, are very helpful in accomplishing these important ends. Yet our experience of such gatherings was, for the most part, singularly uninteresting and even dull.

Here is a sample. It is announced in the church on Sunday that, on the following Thursday evening, there is to be a sociable at the house of Mrs. ——, to which the members of the church are cordially invited. Thursday evening comes, and at 8 p.m., the appointed time of gathering, we find our way to the very respectable and handsomely-furnished house of Mr. and Mrs. ——. Open doors admit us to

brilliantly-lighted and well-heated parlours; where
Mr. and Mrs. —— meet us, and kindly bid us
welcome. Then follow recognitions, and greetings,
and hand-shakings, and introductions; and sundry
observations about the keenness of the wind, and the
depth of the snow, and the position of the mercury
in the thermometer, when the next new moon is to
be, and the probabilities of a change in the weather.

Then there are listless saunterings through the
parlours, mute pauses; vacant gazings upon hand-
somely-bound books, pictures, and ornaments; until
one's dulness is a little bit varied by an ill-selected
and worse-executed tune upon a really splendid
piano. Small observations there are, now and
then, on the state of trade, the Falls of Niagara,
or the surpassing wonders of the far-famed Yo-
Semité Valley; while confused sounds of loud
talking and screaming laughter emanate at intervals
from a circular coterie of matronly ladies, who are
benevolently cutting, and clipping, and stitching
for the poor. Religious matters, too, are occasionally
the subject of remark, though not in a strained
and formal manner.

But, as in most large gatherings all over the
world, there is little worth calling conversation;
and when at 10 p.m., after the reading of a lesson
from the Bible and prayer, the assembly breaks
up, one feels as pleased as a boy who exchanges
the humdrum monotony of a dame's school-room
for the open air and the exhilarating influences of
a familiar circle and home.

A series of missionary services enables us to hear some really able sermons, and to witness much noble generosity in behalf of the glorious missionary cause. With the severely humorous caution of one of the ministers to his people who are to be appealed to on the following Sunday, we are somewhat amused. "Come," says the good man, "*well* prepared to give. Bring your money, and don't lay it down with a *grudge*. When you are putting it on the plate"—here the speaker contracts the muscles of his face, uncovers his teeth, stretches forth his arm, and energetically clenches his fist,— "When you are putting it on the *plate, I say*, don't hold it so *tight* as that it'll *s-q-u-e-a-l* when leaving your hand."

But we are surprised to find that, so far as we can learn, there is no systematic mode of collecting missionary funds during the course of the year ; and the missionary meeting, which is addressed by an able deputation,—including the gifted and accomplished Dr. Eddy, who has since passed in peaceful triumph to his reward,—is thinly attended, flatly unenthusiastic, and excludes from its programme a collection for the funds. This last surprises us a good deal, as the American people are generous, and almost always make collections at their religious gatherings, often not excepting the week-evening prayer-meeting and even the Sunday-school.

CHAPTER XIII.

TIME flies, the sun grows warmer, the ice melts, the Hudson is free ; and, as the navigation is now open, we set out by steamboat for the city of New York. And a noble river-steamer this is,—large, comfortable, richly furnished, and with admirably neat sleeping apartments that are commodious and clean.

Of this majestic river we see little ; for we start in the evening, and soon all things,—towns, villas, trees, and skirting fields,—are wrapped in shade. Night brings us sleep, and ere we wake in the morning our steamer is lying motionless at the pier in New York. After a brief stay with kind Mrs. ⸻ and her interesting and worthy family, we, in company with a much-valued friend, transfer ourselves by rail to Paterson in New Jersey.

This is a rapidly-growing city, with a goodly number of handsome private residences, some of which belong to merchants who transact their business in New York. The population is about forty thousand, and is increasing rapidly year by year. But trade just now is bad, and many of the operatives of the place are receiving help administered by a well-organized committee ; the chairman of which is an old and esteemed acquaintance whom we had formerly known in the Emerald Isle.

We put up with a lady and gentleman from the Southern States, both of whom are as polite, kind, and attentive as one can desire. The Methodist Conference is in session ; but, as all American conferences are conducted in the same way, there is scarcely anything new to observe.

At a meeting held in behalf of the Freedmen's Aid Society,—a noble institution, that has for its aim the education and religious training of the five millions of newly-emancipated coloured people in the South,—a certain doctor excites our risibility by giving us the following bit of his personal experience. He was down South, had preached, and was heard by a religious negress. This woman, on going home, tells her master much in praise of the preacher. To other laudatory statements she adds :—" O, massa, him be *great* preacher ! Him be *berry great* preacher ! O, massa, massa, him be *berry*, BERRY great preacher ! Him be *sounding brass and tinkling cymbal !* "

Another doctor, speaking on the subject of Christian liberality, informs us as follows. At one time, a man imbued with Baptist notions came to him that he might be baptized. But before having the rite administered to him, he questions the doctor as to his authority to do so. "I have full authority to do so,"—replies the doctor,—"for I can trace my pedigree as far back as John the Baptist. I have been connected in a direct line with Roger Williams ;

and you know that you Baptists believe that Williams could trace his pedigree to John the Baptist, and if Williams could trace his pedigree to John the Baptist; and I can trace my pedigree to Williams, it follows that I can trace my pedigree to John the Baptist too." The man is satisfied; and, as he is to be baptized by immersion, he commences to remove some of his appurtenances, and, amongst others, his purse. "That won't do,"—says the doctor;—"leave that purse where it is. You must be dipped, *purse and all.*" And so he was; and, from that day forth, that baptized purse was always open to help a good cause. The doctor concludes by urging upon his audience the need of getting their purses baptized.

At one of the sessions a collection is made after the fashion already noticed in another part of this work. The presiding Bishop wants five hundred dollars for some charitable institution in the South, requires the money very much, must have it, won't take less, must have it on the spot.

Then commences the auctioneering style of competition in giving, and in announcing the number of dollars given. Round and round goes the *hat*, and round and round again; and at the end of about half an hour, during which the greatest good-humour prevails, the sum of five hundred dollars is actually raised. The benevolent Bishop is delighted and thankful, and every one else seems heartily pleased.

On the following Sunday, we hear this same Bishop preach a luminous and powerful discourse to a large, a respectable, and a deeply-interested audience.

Other members of the Conference occupy pulpits belonging not only to their own denomination, but to the Baptists, Presbyterians, and others ; for in America there is little of that sectarian narrowness, bigotry, and intolerance that are so disgraceful to us.

But what a piece of child's play this is. A minister present has a gold watch presented to him in the Conference. It is the gift of the people amongst whom he has recently laboured ; and it is conveyed by a certain doctor, who introduces the affair with an ingenious sensational preliminary speech. Of course, the modest recipient receives it with proper grace. But who could suppose that this same watch had been duly presented by this same people to this same minister on another occasion a short time before ; that it had been accepted by him ; and that it had been given back (we suppose at the request of the givers) by the recipient, for the purpose of having it presented to him in the presence of the Conference again. Yet such, we are credibly informed, had been really the case.

At a "Church extension" meeting of very great importance and interest, it sounds strange to us to hear Chaplain M—— called upon for a song. The chaplain is silent. But, again and again, the call is echoed by many voices from different parts of the church,—"A song ! a song !" The good chaplain, willing to oblige, rises from his seat on the platform, makes his bow to the audience, and in loud and full tones, though a trifle husky with cold, he sings throughout the well-known composition beginning with :—

> " To the hall of the feast came the sinful and fair,
> She heard in the city that Jesus was there;
> Unheeding the splendour that blazed on the board,
> She silently knelt at the feet of the Lord."

By the way, this reminds us that we, one time in New York, saw a minister, after sermon, come to the communion rails, and sing for the congregation something similar to the above while the collection was being made. Perhaps he thought it quite as musical as a voluntary performed on the organ, and a good bit more edifying too.

The most remarkable man present at this Conference is a minister in the hundredth year of his age. He is tall and venerable-looking; his faculties are unimpaired; and he engages, if spared till next Conference, to preach his centenary sermon. Wonderful to tell, this engagement is subsequently kept. But let us return to New York, and cross over to

BROOKLYN.

To many persons who have not been in America, Brooklyn is an unimportant place,—in fact, a mere suburb of New York. What an utter mistake! True it is that Brooklyn is a sort of suburban outlet of the great City; for it furnishes residences for multitudes who transact business in New York; and who are glad, after the toils and cares of the busy day, to slip across the ferry to a quiet home in Long Island.

Yet this same suburban outlet is itself a city, containing about 400,000 people, with long avenues of imposing houses, fine squares, and a grand array of lofty and handsome churches. It has a fine park also, through which we have the pleasure of a drive ; and it has more than one extensive, handsome, and well-kept cemetery.

Of these last, the principal is Greenwood. Indeed, Greenwood Cemetery is, perhaps, the finest in the world. In this solemn resting-place of the dead are acres upon acres of beautifully laid out grounds ;— sometimes lying flat in shaven lawns, sometimes undulating amid the peaceful shades of lofty trees or luxuriant and variegated shrubbery, sometimes gleaming with the sheen reflected from spouting jets or broad patches of tranquil and transparent water ; and everywhere decked with monumental marbles, whose pyramidal tombs and graceful statues are set in squares and circlets of living flowers that are ever nurtured by the careful and gentle hand of afflicted and sorrowing love.

As we pace the smooth and ever-curving walks, or slowly climb the grassy mounds, or loiter in the shade, or, with admiring gaze, ponder some beauteous work of chiseled art, we are filled with pleasing wonder. But uprising, like a black cloud upon a summer sky, comes the doleful thought :—this is but the tinselled pomp, the gorgeous mantling of hideous and inexorable Death.

Yet death is not, as the atheist would have it,— an eternal sleep. A sleep, indeed, it is, and a deep sleep and solemn; but it is not eternal. Nor is it even a temporary sleep for the living, though departed, soul; else no voice from heaven should proclaim, — "Blessed are the dead which die in the Lord from henceforth : Yea, saith the Spirit, that they may rest from their labours; and their works do follow them." Nor should the yearning spirit of a great apostle have prompted him to say,—"Having a desire to depart and be with Christ, which is far better." But we may not linger in the habitation of the dead.

The New York East Conference of the Methodist Episcopal Church is in session. Let us go and have a glimpse. The place of meeting is a handsome and commodious church, and the number of assembled ministers is large. The presiding Bishop seems a remarkably placid, yet intellectually vigorous, man ; and never, by anything arbitrary in conduct or unseemly in language, temper, or manner, compromises either his own dignity or that of the assembly over which he presides. Small matters are quickly despatched ; while affairs of importance are fully and freely debated, and with considerable skill. To us this Conference seems to contain an unusually large number of able men. There is a large attendance of the public, too ; occupying both the galleries and a good part of the floor of the church, and seeming to watch the proceedings with very great interest and zest.

But a scene occurs that leads us to doubt the wisdom of indiscriminately admitting the public to the Sessions of Conference. While business is going on, a man suddenly rises in the middle of the church, and commences a violent harangue against the Methodist people; appealing most vociferously to the Conference against the conduct of certain trustees, who, he alleges, have grievously wronged him. An effort is made to silence him; but in vain. Several efforts of a similar nature follow, with cries of,—"Stop him,"—"Put him out,"—"Send for a constable." Yet the intruder continues speaking at the top of his voice, and in a very excited manner. Much confusion follows. At length, one of the brethren hits upon an expedient. He raises the hymn, commencing with,—"All hail the power of Jesus' name!" A good many voices join in, and the voice of the intruder is drowned. The singing ceases, and again the disturber begins. But the appearance of one of those gigantic New York policemen—many of whom are Irish, and are by the New-Yorkers facetiously called *infants*,—making his way through the assembly, cools the courage, abridges the argument, and annihilates the vocal power of the injured hero. We think it right, however, to observe that the expedient of putting the unruly stranger down by singing a hymn originated in unthinking impulse, was not participated in by the majority of the ministers, and, we have reason to believe, was subsequently condemned by them all. If there must be open Conferences, and very many are of opinion that there should be, the doors ought to be guarded in some way, so that all sorts of folks may not be permitted to enter, and, possibly, by some kind of interference, to abuse the privilege of being permitted so to do.

A, to us at least, rather novel discussion takes place on the subject of printing in the Minutes of Conference the obituaries of deceased wives of ministers. Many of the remarks made are sensible and touching ; but one of the speeches puts our gravity to a serious test. A good brother, strongly advocating the insertion of such obituaries, adds with much sorrowfulness of facial expression and deep pathos of voice,—"As for me, I shouldn't like that the memory of my dear wife should perish. No, no ; I should not wish it to be like a meteor that flashes across the sky for a moment, and then vanishes in darkness. No, no ; I should wish it to be like a bright star in the firmament, that shines on and on and on, with undying splendour. Indeed, I often take my *present* partner to visit the grave of my *late* dear partner, as a tribute of my respect for her memory." This last sentence is very affecting, not only to ourselves, but to many others in the large assembly ; especially to the ladies, who are endeavouring to conceal their emotions by putting their pocket-handkerchiefs into their mouths.

During the Conference we hear some good preaching. The sermons, however, are chiefly read ; and one of the discourses,—preached by a gifted man, and intended chiefly for the ministers,—seemed to us much more florid than theologically sound.

On the whole, we greatly admire this Conference.

It is gifted and accomplished; and we are glad to observe that not a few of its worthy members are either of Irish descent or Irishmen by birth.

There are two men in Brooklyn whom we are anxious to hear, both of them men of pulpit renown. Of course, we mean Beecher and Talmage.

To the church of the former we bend our way on a quiet sunshiny Sabbath morning ; and, as we arrive there long before the time of beginning the service, we feel somewhat disappointed at not being able to get a seat. The truth is, the church, which holds between two and three thousand people, is crammed, while many persons in the street are not able so much as to get near the doors. So, "after considerable of a crush, stranger," during which we have serious fears for the safety of the skirts of our coat, we are very well pleased to get a few inches of standing-room just within the body of the building.

The service is simple, yet beautifully orderly and affectingly solemn. The reading of the Scriptures and the extemporaneous, yet comprehensive and reverential, prayer are all that one can desire. But O, what music!—so chastely simple ; and yet so grandly, solemnly, and touchingly rendered by a sweet, powerful, and skilfully manipulated organ, a numerous and well-trained choir, and the full and harmonious swell and cadence of a multitude of voices, richly and sublimely blending in the lofty, yet lowly, worship of Almighty God.

The sermon is preceded by a long and almost wearisome catalogue of announcements ; some of

N

which, however, are uttered in so droll a way as to tickle the hearers into smiles, and, sometimes, to elicit their audible laughter :—very funny and witty, we think ; but a bad sequel to the worship immediately preceding, and an unbecoming prelude to the solemn utterance of Gospel truth.

The discourse itself does not meet our expectations. The text is splendid, full of evangelical meaning ; but we listen in vain for the evangelical teaching of the preacher. The countenance is pleasant, the voice good, the gesture natural, easy, and agreeable, the utterance fluent, the illustrations apt, the language felicitous and chaste. But where are the barbed arrows to wound the consciences of ungodly men ?—where the balm to heal the broken-hearted ?—where the living streams, the wine and milk to refresh the weary pilgrim as he journeys to the promised rest ?—These are not here.

Having now heard Mr. B—— on several occasions, we can scarcely resist the conviction that his staple germinal ideas are two,—the fatherhood of God and the brotherhood of man. These seem like gravitating centres around which his mind perpetually revolves, and upon which all his thoughts converge, or like ideal founts whence, both for his own and others' comfort, he never fails to draw.

Now these two ideas are good. Indeed, they are grand ; and, like all grand ideas, they have far-extending relations to many other truths, and are amply prolific of other thoughts. Yet they do not adequately represent either God or man ; for God is not only a kind and merciful Father, but He is also a righteous Governor, a Redeemer through Atonement righteously exacted, and a just Judge ; and man is universally and utterly fallen, and is, too often, to his fellow-man as fraternal as Cain was to Abel.

We are told that, in the afternoon, Mr. B—— is to preach a funeral sermon for a man who is to be buried a third time. Twice already this person has been buried with due religious rite, but twice his remains have been exhumed to ascertain if he had been treacherously despatched by poison ; and a third time, as we are informed, Mr. B—— is to preach about, and to bury him again. Curiosity prompts us to witness this strange ceremonial, but our circumstances forbid.

The evening brings us to Talmage's Tabernacle. This is a new Presbyterian church, and as we enter we are much struck with the magnificence of its size, and the costly elegance of its finish. It is an amphitheatre with a deep gallery, seating about five thousand people. The preacher stands on a platform about five feet above the level of the floor, from which he can, with eye and voice, command the entire house. There is no choir ; the singing being led by a powerful organ, and by a precentor, who, standing on the platform, waves, magician-like, his rod. Could not such an automaton-looking official as this latter be done away with ? Perhaps not. But if he could, by all means let him go. For our own part, we think we could keep good time and modulate the

N 2

voice by attending to our book and following the tones of the organ ; and should worship all the more comfortably if our eye were not distracted and offended by the swinging, and bending, and jerking manœuvres of this minstrel-fugleman, who seems to think that all the harmony of the occasion depends upon the service rendered by himself.

The appearance of the preacher is not prepossessing, nor are we fascinated by the hoarse, raven-like tones of his voice. His gesture, too, is negligent to a fault. But, as he proceeds with his sermon, the conviction seizes us,—here is a man indeed; ay, not only a man, but a mighty man of God. What gleaming flashes of truth,—what apt illustration,—what well-directed thrusts at the conscience,—what rebuke,—what a full and vivid display of the bleeding Atonement,—what encouragement,—what persuasive entreaty,—what vehemence of language and manner,—what a rushing cataract of feeling ! Such are some of our thoughts during the short half-hour that we listen to this scribe, so well ''instructed unto the kingdom of heaven.'' To Beecher's church for singing ; but for preaching, by all means to Talmage's Tabernacle.

As the season is now advancing towards summer, a trip by the South Side Railroad to Pachoge, and thence by stage to Belport, gives us an opportunity of seeing much of Long Island.

All along our route we observe that towns and villages are springing up with mushroom growth, many of which are handsome, and rising into import-

ance. We also pass many luxurious-looking rural
residences and pretty villas; with their surroundings
of garden, orchard, and tree-besprinkled field. Yet
much of the country has a rugged and uncultured
look, and we miss a great deal of what is charming
in an English landscape. The grass is beautifully
green, reminding us of the exquisite emerald of our
native isle, and we are much struck with the ample
and snowy bloom of the peach and cherry; but there
is nowhere to be seen the golden leaflet of the scented
furze, the green hedgerow plumed in white, the
dainty little field-daisy, the delicately-yellow prim-
rose, peeping, like a modest virgin, from the moss-
enveloped ditch, or the graceful ivy, clasping with
its tendrils, and entwining and garlanding with
its foliage the venerable oak. Songsters, too, are
scarce; and we listen in vain for the joyous carolling
of the soaring lark, or for the sweet notes of the
blackbird, the thrush, the linnet, and many other
warblers of our meadows, lawns, and groves.

The soil, however, seems to abound with a luxuriant
clover, wild strawberry, and a violet of richest hue.
The mocking-bird salutes us with his strong and
pleasing notes; and a species of robin, nearly as large
as our thrush, utters, at frequent intervals, a melodious
song.

The roads are, of course, greatly superior to those
in the distant West; but the clumsy and rumbling
vehicle is no better than that with which we have
had a painful acquaintance on the Pacific coast.
How strange and contradictory it is, that nothing in

America seems to stand absolutely still, except this dreadful travelling stage. And this is all the more to be wondered at, since the American private carriages are remarkable for their lightness and elegance of build.

In the neighbourhood of Belport, a pretty fishing village whose skirts are washed by the waves of the Atlantic, we are much struck with the appearance of some children whom we happened incidentally to meet. The features are beautifully regular, but the skin is perfectly black and shining. In fact, these little folks seem like handsomely chiseled and highly polished ebony. We are told they are a mixed race, the offspring of Indian and negro parents.

But, leaving Long Island, we return once more to New York, and as we hear a great deal about the religious services of the coloured people, we are desirous of an opportunity to witness their worship. And the opportunity soon offers, for having mentioned our wish to a friend from whose self and family we have already experienced much attention and kindness, he proposes that we go on Sunday next to the morning service to the darkies in B—— Street Church.

The day arrives, and the time of service finds us in the church ; and, fatigued as we are, after a long walk beneath a sun that has made us stream at every pore, we are only too glad to get sitting in a nicely-cushioned pew.

The church is a good one, neatly ornamented, and large, but not nearly full. Indeed, the con-

gregation, all of whom except ourselves are coloured,
are sparsely sitting in the pews below, while the
galleries seem not occupied at all. But the wor-
shippers keep straggling slowly in, a fact of which
we received ample notice by the loud and frequent
creaking of approaching shoes. We observe, too,
that as each person comes in he or she attracts
the attention of others; and this is followed by
mutual recognitions, which show themselves in sharp
glances, broad good-natured smiles, and sundry bows,
with salutatory noddings and shakings of woolly
heads. All are well dressed, with here and there
a little faded finery and showy ornaments of ques-
tionable gold.

The singing is not as good as we expected;
especially as we had lately heard a learned American
doctor, when descanting on the æsthetic genius of
the African race, say that in the course of a few
years the coloured people will have the most beautiful
churches, the finest singing, and the most eloquent
preaching on the American Continent. The singing
here is fair, with a touch of weird melancholy in its
tones; but there is nothing in it to suggest a con-
firmation of the opinion of the aforesaid learned
divine.

The minister—a genuine ebony, with a placid,
and indeed almost smiling face,—is clad in the
customary ministerial garb; with broad shirt-front,
very white, and relieved by a black neckerchief
neatly tied in a sailor's knot. There is great propriety in his manner and language, fervid earnest-

ness in his appropriate extemporaneous prayer, and
solemnity and clearness of utterance in his reading of
the Word of God.

The sermon, which might be preached from almost
any text in the Bible, contains much godly admoni-
tion, warning, and encouragement; but some of the
sayings of the preacher compel us to smile; while,
occasionally, the loud, shrill, and almost hysterical
responses of a few of his hearers operate upon our
nerves with something like electrical suddenness and
force. "Religion without love!" ejaculates the
good man, — "Religion without love! Religion
without *love!* Why"—here he snaps his fingers
with an energy that the Americans are fond of
calling *vim,*—"it ain't worth a *snuff!*" Again,
he declared,—"As for me, I intend to preach the
truth; for I know *nothing better* than the truth."
—"Ay, ay! That's right! Preach the truth!"—
respond a number of voices in different parts of
the building, and in loud echo-like succession. Soon
after, the preacher becomes a very little bit excited,
and speaks, almost without any emotion, of "Glory;"
upon which a regular gust of audibly expressed
feeling sweeps over the audience, accompanied by
a great display of white handkerchiefs, bowing of
heads, and wiping of eyes; whilst a good woman
just behind us gives such a loud scream-like shout
as makes us literally jump from our seat.

All this subjects us to feelings of considerable
pain. We want to be serious. Indeed, we try hard
to be so. But the thing is so strange,—there is so

great an effect from so small a cause, so great a
demonstration with so little to evoke it,—that the
affair seems unaccountable, surprising, ludicrous.
We feel it is very unseemly and wrong to laugh, and
yet we feel as if we must laugh; although we have
been forewarned before coming to the place that the
penalty of laughing is expulsion from the church.
What can we do ? We almost wish we hadn't come.
Besides, we fear that what we have witnessed may be
only the prelude of such a storm as we have heard
sometimes takes place in the religious meetings of
these people ; and if it shall turn out to be so, our
gravity, which has been so sorely tried by the first
blast of the tempest, must certainly start from its
moorings and be totally and disgracefully wrecked.
Happily for us, however, the emotion subsides as
quickly as it arose, and our serenity is not further
disturbed to the end of the sermon.

But we are forcibly reminded of what we have
heard ministers of considerable experience and
eminence say in New York,—namely, that it is not
possible that coloured people and whites can be
amalgamated in the churches, or that they can
comfortably unite in the same solemn acts of
religious worship.

The sermon ended, another coloured minister, who
has been sitting behind the brother who has preached,
and who is the Pastor of the flock, comes to the front,
and delivers to his people a sort of pastoral charge.
Amongst other things, he says :—" To complete
some improvements which I have been making in this

church, the Bishop has thought it right to send me back a fourth year." Several of the darkies look sharply at each other across the seats, seem serious, and exchange significant nods. "Some of you," continues the Pastor, "won't like this. I know you won't." Again the darkies glance at each other and exchange nods. This time, however, there seems a more fiery sparkle in their eyes. "But," adds the pastor, "whether you like it or not, I can't help it. You know I always behaved myself among you as a Christian and a *gentleman ;* and so long as I'm with you I'll try and do my *duty.*" Then the darkies look less fiery, glance less sharply, and cease nodding their heads. The singing of the doxology, followed by the benediction, brings the service to a close.

Certainly, these negroes are in many respects peculiar. Yet they are an interesting people, and not a few of them are deeply earnest and very intelligent Christians. And although they are sometimes spoken of as lawless and difficult to manage, we have never seen them behave with less moral propriety than others who pride themselves on superiority of race.

CHAPTER XIV.

HOME.

HAVING seen much of America, we resolve to bid her farewell, and once more to trust ourselves on old Neptune's domain. Regardless, however,. of the mythical god whose care upon the ocean voyagers of old invoked with many idolatrous rites, but for whose imaginary majesty,—thanks to divine Revelation,— we care not a straw ; we commend ourselves to the providential keeping of Him whose " kingdom ruleth over all," and " who hath measured the waters in the hollow of His hand."

Our ship, reported to be a splendid sailer, is moving from the pier. Fragrant June smiles in one of her sunniest moods ; and, as we stand on the hurricane-deck, warm-hearted friends waving fare-well, forests of colour-flying masts, and the mighty City, with its masses of houses, its spires, its domes, and its million of busy souls, are slowly receding from our view.

And among those who stand on that retiring pier are B——, and C——, and M—— ; the first, a dear relative, and the other two friends of noblest type. One by one, City and villa-crowned height, and massive fortress, and foam-fringed beach glide away, like charming scenes in a glorious panoramic view ;

and soon again we are amid the watery wastes, beneath an azure canopy of sky.

Our company, with few exceptions, are not such as we could wish; but the accommodations of the ship are ample, the officers courteous and obliging, and the weather splendid. Besides, our rate of sailing is so satisfactory as gives us pleasing assurance that in a few days we shall have skimmed across the rolling waters of what our witty cousins are pleased to call "the pond."

But fine weather does not assure us against accident. Once our machinery gets over-heated and disordered, and obliges us to halt about midway on the deep. At another time we are startled by fire; which, however, by the good providence of God, and by the prompt exertions of officers, passengers, and crew, is speedily extinguished.

One mishap is deeply afflicting. As we pace the deck on a bright afternoon, there is a rush of sailors to the stern, in whose countenances are strongly depicted hurry and alarm. "What," we ask, "is wrong?" To which it is hastily answered—"Man overboard." And so, alas, it is; for, on running aft until we get right above the screw, we catch a glimpse of a fellow-mortal who is drifting helplessly and rapidly astern.

With alacrity,—and yet, now seconds seem like leaden-footed hours,—a boat is partly untied and partly cut down and lowered to the flood. Speedily she is manned by a noble crew. Meantime, a stout young fellow, one of the ship's company,

partly undressed, plunges headlong from beside us
into the undulating wave ; vainly endeavouring to
reach the victim of the sad disaster. The ship,
which has been going at the rate of twelve knots
an hour, takes some time to put about, during
which the drowning man, the swimmer, and the boat
are all left behind.

After a fruitless search and much delay, the boat
returns; bringing the man who had plunged from
beside us into the heaving sea, but not the "man
overboard;" of whom there could not be found a
trace except his hat, and who is gone for ever!

Unhappy victim of intoxicating drink! We had
seen him in the ship just as she left New York. He
was then drunk, noisy, and bleeding at the face;
and, we were told, was returning for the purpose
of seeing his friends in his native land. On the
intervening days we had lost sight of him. Now,
we are informed that he continued drinking in
the ship; until, maddened by the demon that burned
in his veins and brain, he rushed frantically to the
steamer's side, and dropped hopeless into a dismal
ocean and a drunkard's grave.

It is probable, from what we have heard, that the
miserable being who has thus perished was drugged
and robbed in some low lodging-house in New York;
for he was put drunk and bleeding, . and indeed
insane, on board the ship ; and, though he was
returning to see his friends, we learn that he had
neither money nor a vestige of baggage—a condition
in which we can hardly think he could be, unless he

had been subjected to foul play before leaving the
shore.

But who on board the ship supplied that man with
strong drink ? Who was it that thus put his bottle to
his neighbour's mouth ? Whoever that man is, he
should excite not only our indignation, but our
deepest pity ; for all the water in this mighty ocean
cannot wash away his guilt. A wretch, indeed, was
he who, driven frantic with drink, rushed to destruction, and sank into the ocean—

> "———————— Depths with bubbling groan,
> Without a grave, unknell'd, uncoffin'd, and unknown."

Is he less a wretch who supplied him with the
liquor that first maddened him, and then sent him
headlong to perdition ?

As we draw towards the end of our voyage, some
Americans on board are much surprised and pleased
at the length of the day, and at the reluctance with
which the lingering twilight bids a gentle farewell to
the slowly fading sky ; for in the United States
the day is shorter than ours in summer, but longer
in winter, and the twilight is of brief duration.
Our transatlantic friends are much delighted with
the Irish coast, as the broken mountain-outline of its
northern shores comes slowly into view. The emerald
verdure of its soil also attracts their admiring eyes ;
and, with amusing *naïveté*, they ever and anon
exclaim,—"Splendid ! Splendid !—Why ; did ever
we think Ireland was so fine a place as this ?"

But one gentleman in particular,—who has been

raised in a Western city, is a representative of the
press, is full of talk, full of knowledge, brimming
with intelligence, and ever ready to inform and
explain,—is much interested as we approach the
Derry coast. Nearly all the voyage he has been
occupied in smoking, card-playing, and (with
pedantic garrulity) airing his vast acquisitions of
knowledge, on every conceivable topic, for the
benefit of others ; and, now that he is approaching
the shore, he is obligingly and benevolently busy in
explaining every object that comes in sight, and in
kindly enlightening the darkness of all the ignorant
people about him.

"What is that ? "—asks a gentleman, addressing
himself to a group of three or four passengers who
are standing near him on the deck, as the tolerably
well-preserved ruin of a feudal castle comes in view.
" What's what ! "—interjects our lively and well-in-
formed agent of the press, as he comes up in
impatient haste, and directs his keen eye to the
antique building on the shore. And then, without
waiting for reply, he adds,—" Why, that's a round
tower." We, who are standing by and listening,
venture to observe, we think not. "O, but yes, it
is, "—replies this instructor of the people,—" that
is one of the ancient old round towers of *Oirland,*
about *three hundred years* old." Well, but "—we
say—" it isn't round at all ; don't you see 'tis
square ? " "Well, well ; no matter," rejoins the
man of letters,—"I don't care : it is one of the
old round towers." Of course, we say no more.

Soon we are transferred to a tender, which brings
us to the quay in Derry. Here, without the accommodation of shed, platform, or an inch of standing-room beyond the crowded little boat, amid
indescribable confusion, and surrounded by land-
sharks—our luggage is opened, tumbled, and examined by custom-house officials. What a disgrace
to our Government to subject all in-comers to such
a test as this. By all means let them search for
smuggled commodities and wares ; but let them, in
common justice, provide fit accommodation for such
a search, and not subject those whose baggage is
examined to serious inconvenience, injury, and the
possible loss and plunder of their goods. How different
we found it in New York, where there is ample and
unmolested wharf accommodation for such a search.

As we hasten on to Dublin, how small yet beautiful
everything, save the dingy by-way of the town and
the dirty rural cabin, seems. Before going to
America we did not conceive how large America is.
Yet, by degrees, while dwelling there, the idea of its
vastness almost vanished from our thoughts. But,
until our return, we did not know how small Ireland
is. Its rivers seem streams over which we fancy we
could hop, its loftiest elevations seem mountains in
miniature, and its well-fenced fields seem like squares
upon a chess-board. Yet its splendid roads, fringed
with luxuriant hedgerows, its meadows, its lawns, its
moss-grown ditches with rich enamelling of wild
flowers, its crumbling remains of feudal chivalry and
mediæval piety, the floral beauty of its trim gardens,

the gentle slope of its cultivated hills, with their background of hazy mountain and soft blue sky, the rippling music of its crystal streams, the frondal forms and verdure of its joyous groves, its whitewashed cottages, and snug villas ;—all these, and a thousand other landscape beauties, seem as if we had never noticed them before, and fill us with admiration and delight.

THE END.

www.ingramcontent.com/pod-product-compliance
Lightning Source LLC
Chambersburg PA
CBHW030834270326
41928CB00007B/1049